HPBooks

BAGELMANIA
The "Hole" Story

Connie Berman & Suzanne Munshower

AN ULTRA COMMUNICATIONS AND MOUNTAIN LION BOOK

ANOTHER BEST SELLING VOLUME FROM HPBooks

Publisher:	Rick Bailey
Executive Editor:	Randy Summerlin
Editorial Director:	Elaine R. Woodard
Editor:	Patricia J. Aaron
Art Director:	Don Burton
Managing Editor:	Cindy J. Coatsworth
Typography:	Beverly Fine
	Phyllis Hopkins
Director of Manufacturing:	Anthony B. Narducci
Cover Design:	Paul Fitzgerald

ULTRA COMMUNICATIONS AND MOUNTAIN LION

Book Design:	Bobbi Rosenthal
Design Assistant:	Hans Balke
Illustrator:	Rosemary Slader

Published by HPBooks, a division of HPBooks, Inc.
P.O. Box 5367, Tucson, AZ 85703   602/888-2150
©1987 Ultra Communications, Inc., and Mountain Lion Books, Inc.
Printed in the U.S.A.
1st Printing

Library of Congress Cataloging-in-Publication Data

Berman, Connie.

Bagelmania : the "hole" story.

1. Bagels.   2. Cookery (Bagels)   I. Munshower,
Suzanne.   II. Title.   III. Title: Bagel mania.
TX770.B35B47   1987   641.8'15   87-14948
ISBN 0-89586-624-2

With appreciation to Scott Helm and Doug Arnold of Arnold Advertising for their invaluable assistance in the research of this book. . . .and with thanks and antacids to all who contributed their favorite recipes and bagel memories.

CONTENTS

SECTION 4

THE WELL-DRESSED BAGEL

SECTION 5

RECIPES

THE BREAKFAST BAGEL

THE COCKTAIL BAGEL

ROADSIDE AMERICA BAGELS

BAGELS INTERNATIONALE

SECTION
1

BAGEL-MANIA

The roll with the hole that's sweeping the country.

THE BIRTH OF THE BAGEL

Love is sweeping the country, love for a homely little roll with a hole where its middle should be. Bagelmania is here, and it's spreading faster than cream cheese on freshly baked bagels!

Every day, from Hyannis to La Jolla, from Nome to New Orleans, bagelmaniacs (aka "bagel mavens") are gobbling up 8,000,000 bagels! That's a lot of dough! But then, bagelmania crosses all sexual, ethnic and religious borders. Bagelmania is boundaryless and boundless!

And yet, bagelmaniacs do have two things in common.

One, they get a glazed look in their eyes when they speak about the special culinary qualities of the bagel. Two, they're generally stumped by questions about the origin of the bagel.

Just listen to the confusion that arises when bagel-lovers are asked "Where do you think the bagel came from?"

"It must be from Israel, since it's an ethnic food."

"Bagels are German—didn't they used to be called *deutsche* bread?"

"I'm sure they're Polish."

"The bagel? Shoowah, comes from right here in Noo Yowk."

"Didn't they start in California? I thought *everything* did!"

Let's face it, fellow bagel mavens. When it comes to the bagel's origins, most of us don't know enough to fill that little hole in the center.

The truth is, no one really knows where the bagel came from.

No one knows when the first baker decided to take a pile of gluten flour, add water and yeast to make a dough, fashion the dough into doughnut shapes, dunk them in boiling water, then bake them until they were wholesomely browned on the outside and chewy beneath the crust. It's a mystery, the only sure thing being that fire came first.

There are those who even challenge the most commonly held bagel notion—that its origins were Jewish.

Cookbooks and encyclopedias generally credit an unknown Viennese baker with fatherhood. According to this history, the first bagel rolled into the world in 1683, when a local baker wanted to pay tribute to Jan Sobietsky, the King of Poland. King Jan had just saved the people of Austria from an onslaught of Turkish invaders. As the King was both an avid

WANT SMOKED SALMON?

DON'T ASK FOR LOX!

Every bona fide bagelmaniac knows there's "lox" and there's "nova" but most people don't know the difference and call them both "smoked salmon."

That's not true.

Lox is saltier than nova, and the reason is because lox is salted, *not* smoked. Lox is salmon which has been "cured" by being soaked in salt for several days. Nova (short for Nova Scotia salmon) is the salmon that's genuinely smoked. And the crème de la crème is neither lox nor nova—it's smoked salmon from Scotland.

and accomplished horseman, the baker decided to shape the yeast dough into an uneven circle resembling a stirrup.

This theory has merit on two counts. First, the traditional hand-fashioned bagel remains less than perfect in shape. Lacking the doughnut's symmetry, it skews into a shape aptly described as "stirrup-like." Second, the Austrian word for "stirrup" is *beugel*.

Another theory? Well, there's the fact that *beugen* means "to bend," so bagels were invented in Germany.

The Polish explanation has the birth of the bagel in Cracow, Poland, in 1610, where it was created as a delicacy for Cracow's humble, impoverished Jews, normally resigned to a diet of black bread. One of the

few ancient bagel facts is that bagels were mentioned as far back as the 1610 Ordinances from Cracow.

Leo Rosten, author of *The Joys of Yiddish*, also sets the creation of the bagel in 16th century Poland. But he says that bagels then were first made to give to expectant mothers for good luck during childbirth. The idea was that the bagel signified the never-ending circle of life. (Of course, in those pre-Lamaze days, it might have been intended to keep the woman's mind off the pain of labor— "biting the bagel," as it were.)

In the book *Menu Mystique*, Norman Odya Krohn, in discussing Russian *bubliki*, says "This is the name for the original bagel that was made famous in Russian song and rhyme . . ." Strung on strings, they were sold at Russian fairs and were believed to bring good luck.

Wherever it may have appeared first, the bagel's name as we know it today slowly evolved; based on the Yiddish verb *beigen*, meaning to "bend," the roll with the hole was called a *beygel*.

MADE IN THE U.S.A.

The bagel persevered and flourished in Europe for a few centuries before heading for foreign shores. When it finally came to America, it traveled humbly, in steerage. Once in America, the bagel stopped first at Ellis Island, brought by Jewish refugees leaving Eastern Europe shortly after the turn of the 20th Century.

The destination for most of the emigrants was New York City, and here the bagel settled. From the Lower East Side to the farthest reaches of the Bronx, Jewish bakers set up shop. Their customers were, for the most part, fellow refugees, whom they provided with the traditional, beloved baked goods from the Old Country: eggy *challah*, unleavened *matzos*, and, of course, the hardy bagel. Here was born the bagel's reputation as an ethnic "deli" food.

The bagel baker's life in the old days was a far cry from idyllic existence. Most of the brick hearth ovens in which the

Menu Bagelmania!

As the bagel keeps rolling along, it's rolled right up to the top of restaurant menus across these United States. According to *Restaurants & Institutions* magazine, only 12.2% of all U.S. restaurants listed bagels on their menus in 1975. By 1985, that figure had jumped to an impressive 31.3% and was quickly closing in on doughnuts and coffee cake, both of which had dropped below their previous ratings. It's a bagel blitz!

bagels were baked (often at temperatures of 500°) were set up in dark, poorly lit tenement basements, which turned into steamy sweatshops as the bagels were dipped in cauldrons of boiling water. Reminiscing in 1963, Israel Weiner of the Tri-Boro Bagel Company in Fresh Meadows told *The New York Times'* Sidney Schanberg (who later wrote *The Killing Fields*), "In the old days in the cellars, with those coke ovens, it got so hot we used to go around in our underwear."

The bakers weren't the only ones who bemoaned the primitive working conditions. The Health Department wasn't especially happy, either, and were constantly citing the bakeries for sanitation complaints. Small wonder! When the bagelries finally moved to street level many years later, it brought fringe benefits. The bakers made the move because they wanted to expand their businesses, which had always been wholesale operations, but in moving up to street-facilities in order to attract shoppers, they got added benefits. As one baker put it, ". . . no more floods, no more rats, no more mice."

Making bagels by hand meant hard work and long hours. The average trained benchman, the man who kneaded the dough and made the bagels, could twist them out at the rate of a dozen bagels every minute. Then the oven men took over for the actual baking process. In 1960, a thirty-seven hour week paid around $150.00, with the chance to earn up to another hundred dollars in overtime. At twelve bagels per minute, a thirty-seven hour week meant twisting some 25,000 bagels! (Think about that next time you're telling yourself your job's monotonous.)

The men who made the bagels at that time, according to Ben Greenspan of the Beigel Bakers Union, a Local of the American Bakery and Confectionery Workers, were "college students, teachers, lawyers, and other professionals" drawn by the plentiful overtime. Young Americans, and not Old World refugees, were learning the bagel trade.

In the early sixties, a bagel sold for seven cents retail, and a decent-sized bakery such as the Tri-Boro was turning out 140,000 bagels a week. The bagel was still basically a New York City resident at that time, but a family named Lender was already laying the groundwork that would soon have the bagel sweeping the country.

THE BAGEL GETS "LEGS"

There's an old show business expression used to describe a motion picture that's going places in terms of making money. In the language of *Variety*, the property "has legs." Almost every food historian or expert credits one family with giving the bagel the "legs" which would lead to the bageling of America we're now seeing. The Lenders deserve a permanent place in anyone's Bagel Hall of Fame.

Harry Lender was a baker in Lublin, Poland in the early 1920s with a wife, Rosie, and two small sons, Sam and Hymie. Like many Poles, he decided there had to a better world than the one in which he lived, and the country he'd heard so much about—the United States of America—sounded as if it might be the place for him. With enough money to pay only his own passage, Harry left Rosie and the boys behind while he struck out for the land of freedom, opportunity, and, he hoped, appreciation of fine bagels.

Harry docked with a shipload of other emigrants in New York Harbor, but it wasn't long before he'd found a job—baking bagels, of course—at a bakery in Passaic, New Jersey. Harry was a saver and an entrepreneur, so it was only a matter of months before he purchased a baker's lease and equipment in New Haven, Connecticut, all for the princely sum of $1,500.

Harry knew where his talents lay. He converted the 800-square foot conventional bakery into one specializing in bagels, and he soon convinced the other Jewish bakers in town that his product was so superior they should stop baking bagels themselves and buy, instead, from him.

By 1929, Harry could afford to send for his wife and children, putting them to work in the bagel factory. The next year another son, Murray, arrived, followed by Helen and later by the fifth child, Marvin.

In a Depression era, the Lenders did well enough to be able to buy a 1,200-square-foot factory in New Haven by 1934. And yet when Harry thought about the future, he worried. His prospects were limited, with only about 15,000 Jews living in New Haven. And, unfortunately, even *they* tended to nosh bagels Sunday afternoons only. According to third son Murray, "You couldn't bake enough bagels for Sunday, and you couldn't give them away by Monday. It was like Christmas trees on the 26th of December."

Murray joined his older brothers in the family business as soon as he was old enough to help out, even selling bagels outside the Yale Bowl before football games when he was twelve, though he did manage to put in two years at the New Haven College of Commerce. In 1955, Murray's salary was nominally fifty dollars a

THE BIG BUCKS BAGEL CHIP

When David Apfelbaum decided to go into the bagel chip business, he was truly a man ahead of his times, since no machine capable of slicing bagels into chips existed. Standard slicers just weren't up to the job, because bagels are so dense in consistency. A friend helped him come up with a prototype of the world's first bagel chipper, now under patent around the world. No, David's Original Bagel Chips wasn't a company with low start-up costs—$300,000 was shelled out for the original bagel chipper!

week, but the business was rarely doing well enough for him to actually take the money out of it.

Murray shared his father's beatific vision of some day, somehow, introducing millions of non-Jewish noshers to the Lenders' holey roll. Lender's bagels were becoming popular with other ethnic groups in New Haven. Why, Harry wondered, shouldn't there be a way to roll out the bagel farther from home? The family's goal was simple: to find a way to get the bagel out of the neighborhood.

Harry Lender knew he had to come up with a way to cross ethnic lines and get everyone eating bagels. In Murray's words, "It was either that or go out of business."

During 1955 Lender's bagel took its first steps out of New Haven, headed toward the American public at large. It was a small step, but an important one in the Americanization of the bagel. Six bagels were put into a plastic bag; the bags were delivered by a bread distributor to supermarkets throughout the state

of Connecticut and in Massachusetts as well.

The Lenders weren't willing to trust in fate. Sam's wife, Lee, traveled the supermarket circuit, personally handing out samples of bagels with cream cheese to food shoppers.

The supermarket sales climbed, resulting in a heavier workload for the family and indirectly leading them to the key to shipping bagels nationwide.

As the packaged bagels' sales rose, Harry faced production problems. The Lenders were putting in eighteen and twenty hours of grueling work to meet the Sunday bagel rush—and then they'd have to work Sunday night baking up a couple of thousand bagels to fill Monday's deliveries. There had to be some way to trim the time put in.

And so there was. One Friday, Harry had them make extra batches of bagels; then he froze them in an old secondhand freezer he'd purchased. After Sunday baking was finished, the extra bagels were taken out to defrost. The Lenders could now relax—and no one was the wiser.

BAGEL YUKS

Yes, there's actually a bagel joke. According to editor Henry D. Spalding in *The Encyclopedia of Jewish Humor*, it goes something like this:

A Texan visiting New York for the first time decided to sample the dish he'd heard so much about—lox and bagels.

From the first bite, he was in love—so much so that he returned to the same restaurant every day of his two-week stay and noshed on the delicacy.

His last day in town, after he'd finished dining, he called the proprietor over to his table. "I just want y'all to know how much I enjoyed that wonderful dish." he said. "But before I go back to my oil wells in Texas, I wonder if I could ask you a question."

"Sure," said the friendly proprietor. "Go ahead and ask."

"I was just wondering, which is the lox and which is the bagel?"

"We would freeze bagels, defrost them and deliver them as fresh products on the days we weren't baking," Murray revealed much later. "We were originally a seven-day operation in manufacturing and delivery. With the advent of freezing, we were able to shut down the plant on truly slow days—Monday, Tuesday, and Wednesday—and deliver bagels that had been frozen."

There didn't seem to be any reason to tell other folks what they were doing, until Murray forgot to defrost three dozen bagels one morning and delivered them to a delicatessen. Soon the word was out that the Lenders were trying to palm off frozen bagels as fresh. Murray had to do a lot of fast talking to soothe customers; in doing so, he became the natural salesman for the family's products.

Freezing was the answer! Not just to putting in less hours at the factory, but to the Lenders' dream of a bagel in every kitchen in the country. The stumbling block on the road to bagelmania had been staleness, because, chewy and crusty as a bagel is fresh out of the oven, within twelve hours, bagel mortis sets in:

bagel + 12 Hours = Rock

HOW THE BAGEL GOT A HOLE IN THE MIDDLE

Version 1: **Nathan Lippes of Abe's Bagels theorizes the bagel got its hole for practical reasons: so batches of bagels could be strung together for convenience, transport and storage. You mean all this time you thought it was there just so you could pretend you were dieting when you didn't slather the hole with cream cheese?**

Version 2: **Restaurant critic and bagel maven Mimi Sheraton has her own "hole in the bagel" theory. The hole, she says, eliminates the part that would take the longest to bake, thereby keeping the rest of the bagel from burning.**

Since freezing didn't have any serious effect on the bagel's consistency after defrosting, the bagel was now free to travel.

It wasn't long before Lender's products were being regularly sold two ways: frozen wholesale, and fresh retail. But there didn't seem to be a way to combine the two. As much as Lender's Bagels wanted to continue growing, there was no way to get around mass production. Bagel mass production appeared to be out of the question. Too many bakers were needed, and it took a full-year to train a bagel-maker to a skillful standard.

What was needed was automation.

But who'd ever heard of a bagel machine?

There was no such thing. Not yet.

The Lenders searched the U.S. and abroad, trying to find an existing machine that could be redesigned to make bagels as much as possible exactly as they're made by hand. It was impossible. There was no hope of a machine being rerigged to have the capacity to cut dough into strips then bend those strips into bagels.

A variation of the doughnut machine was the final development. The prototype worked along the same lines bagel machines still operate today:

- Flour from 100,000-pound silos was fed into temperature-controlled vats.
- The vats mixed the dough then dumped it onto a conveyor belt.
- The conveyor belt moved the dough to another machine, which divided the dough into small balls.
- Suction cups worked the balls of dough into shape.
- Another machine took over and put the hole in center.

Harry, unfortunately, didn't live to see his dream come true. He died two years before the first frozen bagels were shipped for sale outside the local delivery area in 1962.

ALL THE NEWS THAT'S FIT TO PRINT

Marian Burros, food columnist for *The New York Times*, gives two excellent explanations for the bagel's surging popularity.

"Bagels are fashionable," she says. "They also taste darn good!" Who would object to eating those words?

THE BAGEL:

A Unique Individual

The factor responsible for the bagel's uniqueness is the same factor that makes it so eminently freezable. Other rolls are kneaded, shaped, and baked, but the bagel goes through an extra step—boiling—which, along with the high gluten content of the flour, makes the bagel dense. It's this added density which makes the bagel suitable for freezing.

Think about what happens when you freeze bread. A light, airy-textured bread is never the same after being frozen and defrosted. Its texture doesn't stand up well under low temperatures. On the other hand, dense, heavy breads freeze more successfully. And the bagel freezes best!

Basically, all bagels are made in the same method. The flour is mixed with other ingredients, and leavened with yeast; the dough is kneaded and formed in circles.

Next comes the magic step. The baked bagel is dunked into a vat of boiling, sometimes sugared, water, where it "bathes" for about two minutes. This soaking closes the pores of the dough and is responsible for the smooth, sleek texture of the bagel's crust. The bagel is then baked in a hot oven until the crust turns golden brown. The end product? In her cookbook published in the early 1950s, radio star Molly Goldberg (Gertrude Berg) expressed it this way: "Bagels is a roll. It's more of a varnished doughnut made with special bread dough. It is a thing of beauty to behold, especially on a cold Sunday morning in winter."

Thirty years later the bagel is considered a year-round item, but, just as in Molly's heyday, sales are still highest in the winter months. Of course, back when those words were written by the beloved Jewish comedienne, most *goyim* didn't even know exactly what a bagel even *was* (and her explanation couldn't have helped them a great deal). With time, more and more Americans started seeing those strange, doughy

NAMING THE NOSHERIES

Bagel shops and eateries have names ranging from the forthright (the many outlets of Bagel Nosh) to the fey (our favorite is Johann Sebastian Bagel in Memphis, Tennessee). Here are some yet-to-be-used suggestions for bagelries:

- The Bagel Also Rises (for Hemingway fans)
- The Loxsmith Shop
- There's Nova Place Like Home
- Cordon Bagel
- Somewhere Over the Bagel (in Kansas, please)
- Bageldale's (Bagie's, for short)

rings in the freezer cases at the supermarket and in the display cases at the bakery. They decided to try bagels. They decided they liked them. They became bagelmaniacs. And, as fanatics do, they immediately

formed opinions on the subject of what was right and what was wrong for the bagel.

For instance, there are the bagel purists, most of whom ate their first bagel back in the days when bagels were cheap but not

chic to eat. The average bagel purist has not adapted well to progress.

Here's what Mimi Sheraton wrote in an essay for *The New York Times* upon being served a holeless bagel in a coffee shop

- **Casabagel ("Bake It Again, Sam")**
- **The Bagel & I**
- **The Invasion of the Bagel Snatchers (for sci-fi fans)**
- **West Side Bagel**
- **The Maltese Bagel (howdya think Sidney Greenstreet got so fat?)**
- **The Fox & Bagel (British pub)**
- **The Persistence of Bagelry (Dada hangout)**
- **The Bagel Stops Here!**
- **The Posh Nosh**

bagel purist is that he or she insists the only bagel is the freshly baked bagel. Helmer Toro, general manager of H & H bagels in New York City, which recently opened new outlets in Charleston, South Carolina, and Toronto, Canada, avers, "When it comes to quality, there's nothing like a fresh bagel." And Helen McCully, author of *Things You've Always Wanted to Know About Food and Drink* rather casually mentions in her book the fact that *first-class* bakers still make their bagels by hand.

Needless to say, none of these purists will ever convince Murray Lender, who swears a taste-tester would be unable to tell a defrosted bagel from a fresh one. As for toasting bagels, Murray could tell Mimi this is nothing new, since back in the 1950s when his sister-in-law was handing out free bagel samples in all those supermarkets, she was toasting them before slathering on the cream cheese.

Because of freezing, more people are toasting their bagels than ever before, since most frozen bagels do have a better texture when toasted than

in 1981:

"What used to be a fairly small, dense, gray, cool and chewy delight that gave the jaw muscles a Sunday morning workout had become snowy white, puffy and huge and is now even served hot, or, worse yet, toasted. Stylistically, today's bagel is closer to a brioche or an English muffin than it is to the yeasty, boiled and baked Eastern European original...."

Another characteristic of the

TIME—AND THE BAGEL— MARCHES ON

In 1954, some "canny" entrepreneur came up with an idea whose time never did come and attempted to market *canned* bagels!

During a bagel baker's strike later in the fifties, the union generously kept one bakery operating, just for those folks who couldn't live without a bagel!

In 1960, New York City's 250,000 bagels a day were baked by the 350 members of the Beigel Bakers Union and delivered to delis and markets by the Teamster's 100 bagel deliverers. The delivery men got a special "perk": each man's pay included two dozen bagels per day!

when served simply defrosted. And the freezing process is considered by almost everyone in the bagel industry to be responsible for the bagel's new-found popularity.

"Now that frozen bagels are available in supermarkets," Nate Lippes of Abel's Bagels said shortly after Abel's had expanded into a new 34,000-foot factory outside Buffalo, New York, in 1975, "the average non-Jewish housewife is just beginning to learn what they are. While she was growing up, it was only a word to her, if that much. But her children know very well what bagels are. In emerging from their traditional marketplace, bagels became a youth-oriented food. We are reaching the youth market."

Abel's was founded by Harry Lippes, a third-generation bagel baker who came to America from Rumania in 1913 and opened his one-man bakery in Buffalo. In the 1940s, Abel's made bagel history by introducing the pumpernickel bagel. This was almost the "dumpernickel" bagel, by the way—it bombed at the time, but when reintroduced as a frozen product, the pumpernickel bagel grew "legs."

As for the bagel purists, who insist the only good bagel is a fresh-baked bagel, Murray Lender had, as usual, the last word: "To them, I say if it weren't for freezing, the bagel would probably still be in Brooklyn."

THE BAGEL ABROAD

Though the bagel's growing popularity overseas still can't compare to the fervent reception it's received across America, the European bagel does have the distinction of being one of few foods, if not the only one, which was ever actually banned in a foreign country!

It happened in 1960 in Poland, the land which is the major contender for the title of the The Bagel's birthplace. Most of the Jews had departed from the Polish town of Ostrowiec Swietokrzyski, but the Gentiles who had remained still loved a good bagel. What they didn't like was paying taxes.

Polish bakers, required to pay a tax on every different bakery product they purveyed, officially no longer baked bagels. Why then, the government one day began to wonder, were so many citizens of the town of 36,000 spied noshing bagels in public places

BAGEL QUOTES

Next time someone's bugging you, give the Evil Eye and mutter this old-time Yiddish curse: "Go to hell head downwards and bake bagels."

There's even a bagel aphorism! One of Leo Rosten's favorite folk sayings, which he quotes in *Leo Rosten's Treasury of Jewish Quotations*: "If you eat your bagel, you'll have nothing left but the hole."

throughout the day? They had to be getting them from scofflaw bakers!

Local agents of the Police Militia, frustrated by their vain attempts to crack down on the nontaxpaying bakers, were driven to a desperate measure: *they banned the bagel!*

Not surprisingly, the ban on bagels worked about as well as Prohibition had in the U.S. The self-defined forefathers of bageldom were not about to give up their favorite roll even if it was now forbidden fruit. Bagels went underground in Poland as bootleg bakers foiled the authorities and kept the faithful fed, garnering much public praise from American bagel boosters.

The bagel's fame has spread far beyond its old stomping grounds of Eastern Europe. The British, for instance, have put the bagel right up there with crumpets and scones. Until the late 1970s, the bagel was scarcely seen in the United Kingdom, except in London's East End Jewish neighborhoods, where they were still called "beigels" and pronounced "bye-guls." These rolls bore little resemblance to the Americans' beloved bagel and, in the words of one British bagelpreneur, bore little resemblance to "decent bagels."

David Margulies, a New Jersey businessman relocated to London, was that fellow, and his opening of the American Bagel Factory in London's Edgware Road in 1977 did much to speed the bagel's popularity amongst the Brits.

Margulies, a certified bagelmaniac who wore a gold bagel-shaped lapel pin and belt buckle, sold bagels for nine pence (about 17¢ at the time) each, in eight flavors: onion, garlic, poppy seed, sesame seed, pumpernickel, plain, raisin and cinnamon.

America brought a second bagel wave to England in 1983, when Brooklyn native Ron Stieglitz founded New York bagels.

The time was right for bagel expansion in England as the British began embracing everything American—from hot fudge sundaes to burgers to barbecued ribs and thick shakes—with almost un-British enthusiasm.

New York bagels produced six kinds of bagels—plain, onion, salt, sesame, poppy and pumpernickel—and the British fancied them all, for their uniqueness and their taste of America. As one of Mr. Stieglitz's customers explained, "I eat them for breakfast with salmon and cream cheese, since I was told this is the acceptable practice in New York. I prefer bagels to bread as they're a bit out of the ordinary."

They're more than a bit out of the ordinary in China, where Sidney Shapiro, a former Brooklynite who'd become a Chinese citizen, had to create his own unique recipe—based on Chinese bun dough—to be able to satisfy his bottomless bagel cravings.

Bringing recipes for baked goods across international borders is never a simple task because of the ingredients involved. One reason Italian bread tastes better in Italy, brioche taste better in France, and bagels taste better in the States is because it's impossible to guarantee consistency of ingredients too far afield. Jack Sugarman, "bagel consultant" to David Margulies, found that making a bagel abroad taste as good as the real thing was a stiff challenge. "It's not easy," he confessed, "to bake a good bagel when you wind up in a country where things like flour and water—all the available ingredients except the salt—differ chemically from those in New York."

And yet foreigners want the same foods available in New York. Lyle Fox, an ex-Chicagoan now living in Tokyo, feels the Japanese were eager to try his bagel when he set up shop in Japan in 1982 because the "Japanese associate it with New York, and they associate New York with fashion. A lot of our customers are these young women who consider the bagel as sort of another accessory."

The things the Japanese do with bagels might horrify most stateside bagel mavens: they use them for ham and cheese sandwiches; spread them with a mixture of cream cheese, dried boni-to shavings and soy sauce; ask for lox and cream cheese on a cinnamon-raisin bagel.

The Japanese taste in bagels also varies from the American standard in that they like their bagels smaller, rounder and softer than the New York City version. The important factor as far as Mr. Fox is concerned is that the Japanese are crazy about the darned things! Though he has competition from other bakers (and Tokyo's Jewish Community Center makes its own), Lyle Fox is serving up 6,000 bagels a day, with cinnamon-raisin the hands-down favorite.

THE CROISSANT CONTROVERSY

Meanwhile, those people who wouldn't stoop to bickering about the bagel's size throw their hats in the ring when it comes to campaigning for the bagel or the croissant in the "battle of the breads."

You see, bagel noshers and croissant chompers are two separate breeds, each of which believes that the other is salivating over an inferior food. This is a contest in which perhaps only the bakers of Sara Lee are bipartisan—they've got to be, since their popular frozen croissants are now sharing freezer shelf space with their frozen bagels.

In a classic essay in *The New York Times* a few years back, columnist William Safire attacked the problem. "Of course, a clash was inevitable," he explained. "People whose mouths water at the fragrant flakiness of a croissant turn up their noses at the roundly resistant bagel. For their part, bagel mavens, who have their mouths fixed for the crisp coating and toothsome toughness of the bagel, poke their forks suspiciously at what seems to them to be a greasy, tasteless Danish."

The croissant's crescent shape, according to Safire (with his tongue and not a bagel firmly in cheek), signifies openness to change, while the bagel's sphere stands for the closed circle and traditionality.

The tastes of the croissant crowd and the bagelmaniacs are understandably diametrically opposed. After all, one stands for freshness and flakiness while the other is rooted in solidity and denseness; one leans toward a gentle pulling apart, while the other favors displays of strength. Not only in their choice of means are they opposite; the ends they seek are as distant from one another as Jupiter and Mars, one being ". . . light, flaky, accommodating, digestible" and the other lying ". . .in the stomach like a circular lump of lead."

The croissant may never be as American as apple pie, but it's already ooh-la-la'ed its way into as American an institution as the Roy Rogers restaurant

MOBY BAGEL

Salmon isn't the only smoked fish that makes a delightful companion to a warm, yeasty bagel. Try these:

Sable
Trout
Sturgeon
Chub
Whitefish

And to top off *any* smoked fish on a bagel, add a generous dollop of this horseradish sauce:

1 cup sour cream
1/3 cup grated horseradish
1/4 cup whipping cream
Sugar to taste

Just combine the ingredients in a bowl or blender and chill for at least 1 hour before serving. It's delicious, it's delightful, it's de bagel!

chain. Still, the French import is, let's face it, a tad too airy and flaky for our country's heartland where men are men and women are women and a hunk of dough is expected to sink like a stone once it hits the stomach. In the battle of the breads, the bagel's got the tenacity and the staying power it takes to win out. Denseness is one quality that's never hurt politicians, so why should it keep the bagel from first place?

YIDDISH FOR BAGELMANIACS

You don't have to be Jewish to love bagels. Still, a smattering of Yiddish never hurt anyone! When "shmoozing" about the joys of bagels, these are the words to drop:

nosh—A nosh is any snack that's eaten between meals, but noshing is never a bad thing; the word has only positive connotations.

maven; also *mavin*—If you're a self-defined expert on bagels, you're a bagel maven.

fress—This Yiddish word is exactly the same as the German verb; to fress is to dig into food with great enthusiasm (and also great capacity). If you can bolt down two or three bagels in the blink of an eye, consider yourself a full-fledged fresser!

meichel for the beichel—There's no better way to describe a bagel than this, as it translates into "a gift for the tummy." And when a bagel maven fresses a bagel nosh, it's always a meichel for the beichel!

"YES, VIRGINIA, THERE REALLY ARE PEOPLE WHO HAVE NEVER TASTED A BAGEL"

Most New Yorkers, and other inhabitants of cities with large Jewish populations, would find it hard to believe that folks exist who have never *ever* sunk their teeth into the chewy resiliency of the roll with a hole. But the truth remains: the majority of Americans have never eaten a bagel!

Research varies. One study says four out of five people in this country have never had a bagel. Another says seven out of ten. Still another reports that only 18 to 20 percent of American households consume bagels, with only seven percent purchasing bagels that are frozen.

That's a lot of people missing out on a good thing. But never fear, because America's bagel bakers are doing what they can to remedy the situation. Their enthusiasm for the challenge is awesome.

"We've got 82 percent of the population to tap," Murray Lender announced early in the eighties, speaking in his usual blunt manner. "Once they bite into their first bagel, we know they'll be hooked."

And out in Deerfield, Illinois, a senior vice president of Sara Lee echoed those sentiments, a bit more wordily. Of his company's bagel business, Richard Sharoff said, "It is still in the very evolutional stages of what we think is going to be a pervasive type of bread product for Americans."

Or. . .once you can get consumers to bite a bagel, they're going to go for it in a very big way.

"People are looking for new-and-different"—in the words of Emanuel Goldman, a California consumer analyst—"and for a fair amount of the country, bagels are considered new and different. . . It's really where the growth is, in the non-usual cuisine, like pizza, tacos, bagels, sushi."

INTRODUCING— THE PET BAGEL

Bagels make wonderful pets. Just leave them around for seven days, on your kitchen counter, and they'll become hard as rocks. In fact, almost as hard as the once-popular pet rocks. Pet bagels are easy to care for, require no feeding, don't have to be walked or boarded when you go on vacation and won't shed or bark at your friends. They can "live" anywhere, from a book shelf to a coffee table to a fireplace mantel. Most importantly, pet bagels have an unlimited life span. Like diamonds, pet bagels are forever.

After being acquired by Kraft in 1984, Lender's stepped up its campaign to make every American a bagelmaniac. The market had barely been scratched, but bagel sales were already booming.

Cathleen Toomey, Lender's public relations manager, tried to explain the bagel's newfound popularity in 1985. "It's a result of a broadening public taste," she said. "People travel more and get more exposure to different foods, and they also think more about good nutrition and what they choose to eat. They look for alternatives to white bread. Flavor assortment has also been a major factor in the bagel's rapid acceptance."

If the bagel's popularity continues to spread, it may someday be a staple of the American diet. As Richard Sharoff of Sara Lee said in 1986, bagels are a universal bread. In recalling his company's decision to market the yeasty wonders, Sharoff explained, "Having come off our success with the introduction of frozen croissants, we thought bagels, like croissants, were not just ethnic foods with limited potential. But we think bagels have the making of being even bigger because they are sold for a lower price than croissants. They lend themselves more to everyday eating, while croissants tend to be more special-occasion oriented."

So exactly who's eating all these bagels? Some say the bagel is the new Yuppie nosh, while others believe the bagel isn't upscale enough for upwardly mobile tastes.

Alan Manstoff, who, with his partner Michael Robinson, has begun franchising Chesapeake Bagel Bakery shops (the partners have three shops of their own), says his average customer is 30 years old. In Manstoff's words, "Bagels are real yuppie food."

And the senior vice president of Safeway's 2000 stores says he first guessed bagels would be "the next English muffin" when he noted their appeal to younger shoppers. Cathleen Toomey of Lender's doesn't agree. "We don't feel it is a trendy shift," she told *Public Relations Journal* back in 1985 when discussing the bagel's newfound popularity. "Bagels are not, for instance, a yuppie choice. They are not an expensive item, and yuppies tend to follow a higher-priced, gourmet market."

It would appear that in this case, everyone's right. Yuppies seem to be attracted to bagels in spite of their low price, simply because it's now "in" to rediscover breads which had become obscure. Not only the bagel is having a rebirth. Look at the preponderance of other bread products in chic restaurants which once proferred only classic French rolls or sourdough bread. Muffins abound, popovers have acquired a new elan, and the brioche shows signs of becoming tomorrow's croissant.

Other factors besides fashion account for the bagel's surging sales: nutrition consciousness which has turned Americans against white bread with empty calories; the tendency of more workers to grab a bite at their desk and forget the business lunch, which has increased sales of stuffed foods and sandwiches; the popularity of brunch, for which bagels are almost *de rigeur*.

THE BAGELIZATION OF AMERICA

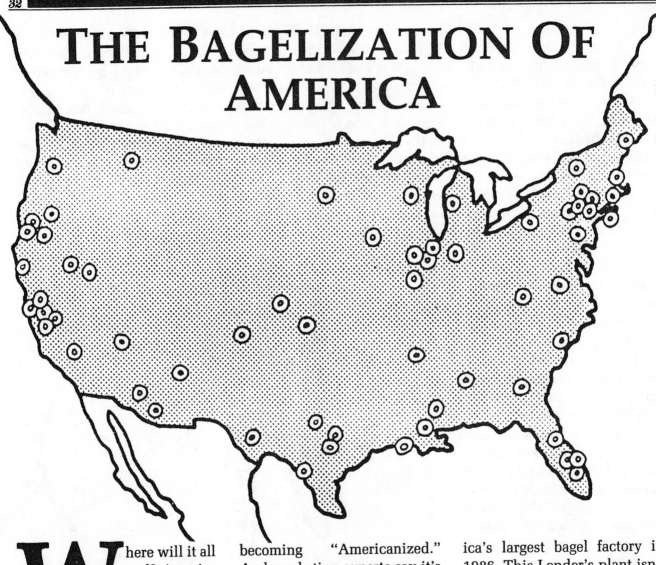

Where will it all end? America is being bagelized, or, as an editor from *Bakery Production and Marketing* trade journal put it, the bagel is becoming "Americanized." And marketing experts say it's only just begun!

One of the highlights of bagel history, second only to the 1984 acquisition of Lender's by Kraft, was the opening of America's largest bagel factory in 1986. This Lender's plant isn't in Brooklyn or on the Lower East Side's Rivington Street; it's in America's heartland, Mattoon, Illinois.

Mattoon, a town of only

THE SUPERMARKET BAGEL

In just a few short years, the bagel boom has brought bagels to almost every town in America big enough to have a supermarket. Safeway sells frozen bagels in all 2,000 of its stores and offers fresh-baked bagels at 850 in-house bakeries. And the Kroger Company, with most of its stores in the Midwest and the South (two longtime non-bagel localities), sells fresh bagels in 85 percent of its 950 stores with bakeries. Lender's alone has its frozen bagels in 30,000 supermarkets. And with a 27 percent increase in frozen bagel sales in just one 12-week period in 1986, we should soon be seeing other major companies trying to cash in on this phenomenal bagel bonanza.

19,800 citizens located 180 miles south of Chicago, is the new bagel capital of the country, with a 14,000-square foot facility boiling up one million bagels a day.

That's a lot of dough. But then, consider the amount of dough Lender's was taking in, impressive enough to make the powers that be at Kraft decide they wanted to call it their own. In 1982, Lender's had net wholesale sales of $39 million; in 1983 this figure had risen to $48 million, and by 1984, sales had soared to $60 million! Combined U.S. bagel sales, say industry experts, now at approximately eight million bagels per day, bring in an estimated $400 million a year.

And it's not only the giants like Lender's and Sara Lee who are raking in the shekels. Thanks to the national advertising campaigns of these two leaders, smaller bagel outlets are also reaping rewards as the bagel becomes recognized anywhere in the United States. Bagel franchises are popping up all over, with many high rollers backing those holey rolls, including R.J. Reynolds Industries. The tobacco conglomerate purchased Skolnik's Bagel Bakery chain, at the time a two-store operation based in Louisville, in 1983. Within a year, they had eleven units in operation, with the promise of triple-digit numbers to come (by June of 1985, they'd added two more units). Other companies do more than just open eateries. For example, Bagel Shoppe, a company out of Maryland, franchises but also sells half-baked or raw bagels wholesale. And since they sold their business to Kraft, the Lenders themselves have been concentrating on expansion of their H. Lender & Sons bagel restaurant chain.

Bagel sidelines have also sprung up, one of the most lucrative being the manufacturing and sales of bagel chips. Salted, unsalted, garlic, onion,

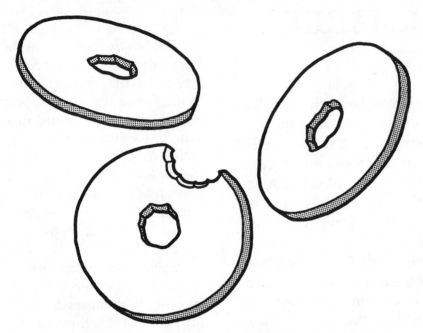

or plain, the bagel chip is now a regular item in both supermarkets and gourmet food shops.

The bagel chip is generally considered to be the commercial brainchild of San Francisco restaurateur David Apfelbaum. "David's Original Bagel Chips" hit the markets in 1983 and sold 14,000 cases of eight-ounce packages in the first three weeks. Apfelbaum spent four years experimenting with bagel chips in the kitchen of his Geary Street delicatessen, working on the proper dough consistency, oil for frying and timing. Then he had to come up with a machine capable of slicing the chips to the ideal thickness.

The result was a product David always knew would be a hit. "I have believed for a long time that there was a way to take the unique flavor and texture of a bagel and turn it into a true snack food," Apfelbaum told the trade magazine *Snack World* in 1984. "For years, neighborhood delicatessens have used up their stale bagels by slicing and toasting them— but that was not the kind of

Want proof that the bagel has definitely broken the ethnic barrier and is considered a strictly Jewish nosh no longer? Try this on for size: the market with the second highest per capita frozen bagel consumption in the country is Grand Rapids, Michigan. That's a long, long way from the Borscht Belt!

WHOSE BAGELS ARE BEST?

It was a historic occasion on November 29, 1985, when the unofficial California Court of Historical Review, established in 1975 to promote interest in San Francisco history, put the bagel on trial. The outcome: the San Francisco bagel was voted every bit as good as the New York bagel.

As the judge noshed, testimony was given by City Treasurer Mary Callinan to the effect that the bagel was brought to San Francisco by miners during the 1849 Gold Rush. Her Irish roots undoubtedly prejudiced her when she stated that the bagel had been created by Saint Patrick and was originally known as the "begora bun."

Callinan was challenged by the former County Supervisor, who called her testimony "half-baked" and implied she'd received "a lot of dough" for her statements on the stand.

But all's well that ends well, and the judge proclaimed the San Francisco bagel equal to the visiting bagel from New York. Besides, he added, the bagel had come to "full maturity" in San Francisco—not seeming to care that remarks like that might make New Yorkers label him "a crumb."

product I had in mind. The bagel is such an honest, natural, eat-anytime good food, and it now crosses all ethnic lines in the marketplace, I'm sure the time has come for a snack version."

With bagel chips in such chains as Safeway and Lucky, David has proved himself to be a true bagel visionary; he also claims to be the inventor of the first "bagel dog" when, way back in the early 1950s, he created a sausage wrapped in a bagel he sold as "The Insiders."

Yes, bagels are everywhere. And they're big business. In 1984, when the Lenders had only two of their now franchised bagel restaurant-bakeries in operation, each seating 110 noshers at 37 tables, the combined gross was $2.6 million. Small wonder that today every mid-size town in America seems to have its own version of a Bagel Nosh, Bagel Shoppe, Bagel Hut or Bagel Box.

The beloved bagel has come a long, long way since it made that long journey across the waters from Europe. But has success gone to its head? No, it's still the same humble, good for any occasion treat for the tummy it's been since its birth back in the Old Country (and who will ever know where?) in the seventeenth century. Today, an estimated 80 percent of all bagel noshers are *goyim*; the days when the bagel was looked upon as strictly an ethnic food are long gone. Bagels are for everyone.

It seems only fitting to leave the last word on the bagel's background to Murray Lender, the acknowledged father of the bagel boom. Just a few years ago he promised he was going to make America "bagel crazy" in a very short time. He's made good that promise—and all we bagelmaniacs are relishing the benefits!

HOW BIG SHOULD A BAGEL BE?

While the Japanese like their bagels on the small side, the American bagel comes in all sizes. As to which is the best or the "right" size for a bagel, there's disagreement galore.

Mimi Sheraton, for one, decries the larger sized bagels often found today because they make it "necessary for two people to share a single bagel, an idea that would have been considered obscene when I was growing up, and unless the eater has a gargantuan appetite, it rules out the pleasant possibility of contemplating seconds."

The traditional bagel weighs in at three ounces. Rob Cagan, the president of WhatsaBagel, a Maryland wholesale and retail bagel company, says his bagel—which weighs in at four ounces and has just a tiny hole in the middle, is the ideal because "Bagels aren't being eaten only with a little bit of butter on them anymore. People want to take them home and put a slab of roast beef, some tomatoes and coleslaw on them. Besides, if people want a bigger hole, they can open it up with their fingers. I give them a bagel that's a meal. If they cut it in half, it's half a meal."

Though Cagan polled his customers and found them to be in favor of the bigger bagel (out of 1,215 people, only 23 would have preferred a smaller bagel), Lender's scoffs at the prospect of the bigger bagel. The two-ounce bagel, says Lender's, is "toaster compatible," a perfect size to pop out of the freezer and into a toaster.

Of course, the purists prefer the three-ouncer because they feel it's the only "genuine" bagel. But the three-ounce bagel, as those of us who grew up B.F.B. (before frozen bagels) can attest to, plays havoc with the average vertical-slice toaster. The toastee usually needs to compress the bagel halves by

THE HOJO BAGEL

Howard Johnson's, those hosts of the heartland's highways, gave in to surging bagelmania and added the wheels of flavor to their national menu in 1984. Did they catch on? Would you believe HoJo's now sells some 16,000 bagels every week? That's what we call *wheeling* and dealing!

mashing them down on a hard surface before they'll even fit into the toaster's narrow bread slots. Then, when the toasting is done, the toastee must invariably unplug the toaster and fish for the bagel with a fork to extract it from the toaster's interior, where heat has caused the halves to expand back to their original breadth.

BAGEL

FACTS &
YOUR
FIGURE

*You can savor their flavor
and not ape their shape!*

MEETING YOUR NUTRITIONAL NEEDS

If you're like most Americans, you are now

■ paying more attention to the food you eat than you did in the past,
■ trying to lose weight or maintain your current weight,
■ cutting back on salt and saturated fats,
■ consuming more fish and fowl than red meat.

Health consciousness has touched every American as more evidence indicates that what we eat strongly influences how long we live and how healthy that life is.

And yet most of us still fall short when it comes to healthful eating habits. For instance, do you eat breakfast? If you don't, you might try starting the day with a bagel. A toasted bagel with peanut butter spread over it and layered with sliced bananas is a high-energy, low-calorie breakfast that will keep you going full steam ahead until lunchtime. And consider this: a ten-year study carried out by U.C.L.A.'s Center for Health Sciences followed nearly 7,000 men and women in California and found that skipping breakfast is among the seven health risks which increase the chances of early death!

The bagel fits right into most people's nutritional needs because it's made with high gluten flour, a specialty wheat flour with a protein content of approximately 41 percent. So the bagel gives the eater an excellent balance of protein and carbohydrate, and, as food and nutrition expert Jane Brody has reported, experiments with high-carbohydrate diets have indicated the value of carbohydrates in painless weight loss because of their ability to leave the dieter feeling satisfied without piling on the calories.

And, if you're a fiber-conscious eater, you can add fiber to your bagel with the addition of banana, celery, cucumber, lettuce, coleslaw or sesame seeds. Of course, if you bake your own bagels, the addition of bran or whole wheat to the dough will also up the fiber content. Because of following a diet lower in carbohydrates than less developed countries, most Americans need more fiber to promote regular functioning of the digestive tract and decrease the chances of developing colon cancer.

Unfortunately, while Americans tend to limit the amount of fiber they ingest, they all too often go hog wild where sodium is concerned. Now, with 320 grams of sodium in a Lender's Plain Bagel, we can't lie and tell you a Pepperidge Farm Croissant has more with 240 milligrams. However, that croissant does have *nine times* the amount of fat as the bagel!

1 beef bouillon cube	960 milligrams
2 slices pumpernickel bread	364 milligrams
8 ounces low-fat cottage cheese	920 milligrams
4 ounces cornbread	545 milligrams
1 ounce Nabisco Wheat Thins	579 milligrams
Burger King Whopper	990 milligrams
McDonald's Filet-0-Fish	781 milligrams
Arby's Roast Beef Sandwich	880 milligrams
Wendy's Single Cheeseburger	1,085 milligrams
2 ounces Shake 'n' Bake	1,925 milligrams
1 level teaspoon salt	2,000 milligrams

Cutting back on sodium is considered invaluable in reducing high blood pressure, and medical authorities also suspect sodium over-indulgence to be indicated in other health problems. And how much sodium should we be eating every day? There's no clean-cut guideline, but most of us need never reach for the salt shaker, since we get more than we need in our food. Here's how daily intakes of sodium could be defined:

200 to 500 milligrams	very low
1,000 milligrams	moderate
2,000 to 3,000 milligrams	liberal

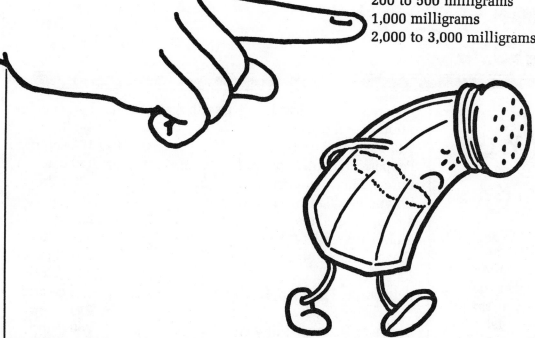

FROZEN ASSETS

Now that they're available in supermarkets from coast to coast, bagels are giving other freezer items a run for their money. In 1985, Americans spent a total of $104,959,000 on frozen bagels in groceries and supermarkets. That's almost half as much as the total spent on all other frozen breads and rolls ($256,638,000) and more than twice as much as was spent on frozen French toast and pancakes ($47,810,000). Considering that these dollars were rung up with only a fraction of Americans embracing bagel culture, it's obvious that thar's gold in them thar holes!

A WORD TO THE WEIGHT-WISE

The bagel is a dieter's delight for two reasons: one, low calorie count when compared to other snack foods, and, it's "stick to the ribs" goodness, a quality which makes half a bagel more filling and satisfying than many more fattening noshes.

Here's how the bagel measures up against some of the competition calorie-wise:

1 (2-oz.) bagel	150-162 calories
Pepperidge Farm Croissant	180 calories
Burger King Whopper	630 calories
Chick-Fil-A Sandwich	404 calories
4 ounces cornbread	235 calories
McDonald's Filet-O-Fish	432 calories
Glazed doughnut	205 calories
Kaiser roll	465 calories
Pepperidge Farm Apple Turnover	310 calories
Strawberry Pop-Tart	210 calories
8 ounces Dannon fruit yogurt	260 calories

Calorie-consciousness means paying attention not just to the bagel itself, but to what you slather on it. When topping your bagel, you may want to take the following caloric values into account:

6 slices cucumber	8 calories
2.5 ounces drained sauerkraut	15 calories
1/4 cup sliced banana	32 calories
1 (1-oz.) slice lean ham	35 calories
1 tablespoon caviar	42 calories
1 ounce pastrami	43 calories
1 tablespoon grape jelly	50 calories
1 ounce sour cream	60 calories
1 tablespoon honey	61 calories
1 (1-oz.) slice beef bologna	90 calories
1 (1.6-oz.) turkey frank	100 calories
1 (1-oz.) slice Swiss cheese	105 calories
1 ounce cream cheese	106 calories
1 tablespoon peanut butter	108 calories
4 ounces crabmeat	115 calories
4 ounces turkey, white meat	132 calories
1 (1.6-oz.) beef frank	150 calories
4 ounces smoked sturgeon	169 calories
4 ounces smoked salmon	200 calories
4 ounces broiled lean ground beef	248 calories

Next time you're heading for a fast-food lunch stand, remind yourself you could be eating a bagel with peanut butter and jelly slathered on it—and consume less than *half* the calories of a Whopper. And that's not even taking into consideration the sodium content of fast foods, which is astronomical.

THE "WATER DOUGHNUT" VERSUS THE GLAZED DOUGHNUT

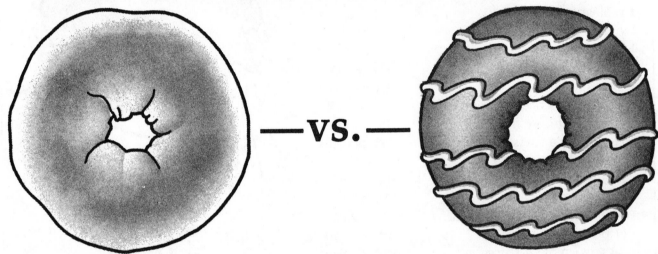

—VS.—

Let's get specific and take an overview of the nutrients in a 3-inch diameter bagel as compared to a 3-3/4-inch diameter glazed, yeast-raised doughnut.

Protein—The bagel supplies six grams of protein for cell-building activities, while the doughnut supplies only three.

Saturated fats—These fats are thought to increase the amount of cholesterol in the blood. The bagel contains only 0.5 grams of saturated fat, while the glazed doughnut contains 3.3 grams.

Carbohydrates—Carbohydrates perform a variety of health duties:

1. supply energy for the central nervous system.
2. spare protein, making it available for building and repairing body tissue.
3. help in the making of nonessential amino acids.
4. prevent dehydration.
5. help form compounds which lubricate joints and form the skin, bones, cartilage and nails.
6. help metabolize fats completely and prevent ketosis (a minimum of 50 to 200 grams per day are needed for this).

The bagel's 28 grams of carbohydrates compare to the doughnut's 22 grams.

Calories—Bagel, 162. Doughnut, 205.

Iron—Iron is essential for the formation of hemoglobin needed to transport oxygen from the lungs to the tissues and carbon dioxide from the tissues to the lungs. It also helps in the transfer of oxygen from the hemoglobin to the muscle cells and in the release of that energy in the cells. The bagel contains 1.2 milligrams of iron, the doughnut, only 0.6 milligrams. The R.D.A. (Recommended Daily Allowance) is 10 to 18 milligrams per day.

Potassium—Our bodies use potassium to maintain a normal water balance and to help control our acid-base balance. Potassium works with sodium in maintaining a regular heartbeat. We need 2.8 grams of potassium per day. The bagel supplies 41 milligrams, the doughnut gives us 34.

Vitamin A—Vitamin A, of which we need from 800 to

QUOTATIONS FOR BAGELMANIACS

"Tell me what you eat and I will tell you what you are."
Anthelme Brillat-Savarin
Physiologie du Gout, 1825

(Bagel-noshers are adaptable, well-rounded and beloved throughout the world. *The Authors*)

"With the bread eaten up, up breaks the company."
Cervantes

(Where bagels are found, company will abound. *The Authors*)

1,000 I.U.s per day, performs three important functions:
1. prevents night blindness.
2. helps in healing of wounds and in maintaining the health of the cornea of the eye.
3. keeps the skin supple and soft.
Vitamin A also promotes bone growth and the formation of tooth enamel in children. The bagel holds 30 I.U.s of Vitamin A, the doughnut, only 25 I.U.s.

Niacin—This water-soluble vitamin prevents pellagra, aids in energy release in the cells, and contributes to proper growth in children. We need 13 to 19 milligrams per day. The bagel gives us 1.2 of these, while the doughnut supplies only 0.8.

Thiamin—Also called Vitamin B1, thiamin helps promote the appetite and functioning of the digestive tract in addition to promoting effective functioning of the nervous system and preventing edema caused by

BAGELNOOK OF THE NORTH

Everyone but everyone loves bagels. Even Eskimos. We've got to be kidding, right? Wrong! The Bagel Deli in Anchorage, Alaska, ships 10,000 bagels a day to Alaska's North Slope area and rural bush country, home of the majority of that state's native Eskimos. Their favorite flavor is onion-poppy, which, of course, goes very well with fish!

impairment of heart function. Of the 1 to 1.5 milligrams needed per day, the bagel contains .14 while the doughnut contains 0.10.

Riboflavin—Also known as Vitamin B2, Riboflavin forms coenzymes important in the release of energy from fats, carbohydrates and proteins. Both bagel and doughnut provide .10 of the 1.2 to 1.7 milligrams required per day.

Obviously, bagels are a better nutritional bet than glazed doughnuts. Bagels are also *all natural*, made without additives or preservatives, which is why they've got such a short (12-hour) life span. Frozen bagels are "blast frozen" fresh from the oven, which gives them a four-month freezer life. But once out of the freezer, even a frozen bagel will take on the consistency of a Pet Rock in 12 hours.

In addition, bagels contain no cholesterol and have a very low sugar content, making them an ideal addition to any diet.

MEASURING THE BAGEL AGAINST OTHER FROZEN MUNCHIES

If you aren't already reading product labels when you shop for groceries, why not start now? You'll learn much more about the foods you're ingesting, and you may end up making some changes for the better in your diet. Be especially alert to sodium content (sodium is often a "hidden" ingredient in low-salt foods through the use of preservatives) and amount of fat. And look for the fiber content (not always listed).

Here's a comparison of the facts and figures printed on the labels of some common supermarket packages:

LENDER'S FROZEN BAGEL (PLAIN)

Calories	150
Protein	6 grams
Carbohydrates	30 grams
Fat	1 gram

Percentages of U.S. RDA:

Protein	10%
Thiamin	15%
Riboflavin	8%
Niacin	8%
Calcium	2%
Iron	6%

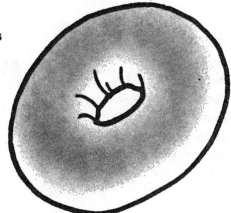

SARA LEE'S FROZEN BAGEL (PLAIN)

Calories	230
Protein	9 grams
Carbohydrates	45 grams
Fat	1 gram

Percentage of U.S. RDA:

Protein	10%
Thiamin	25%
Riboflavin	10%
Niacin	10%
Iron	15%

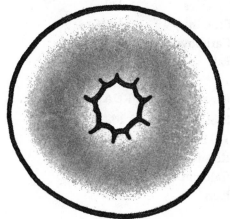

▶

PEPPERIDGE FARM CROISSANT

Calories	180
Protein	4 grams
Carbohydrates	20 grams
Fat	9 grams

Percentage of U.S. RDA:

Protein	6%
Vitamin A	6%
Thiamin	15%
Riboflavin	8%
Niacin	8%
Calcium	2%
Iron	6%

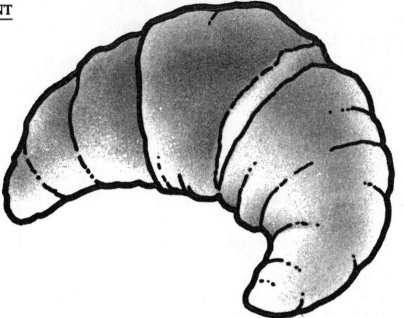

THOMAS' ENGLISH MUFFIN

Calories	130
Protein	4 grams
Carbohydrates	26 grams
Fat	1 gram

Percentage U.S. RDA

Protein	6%
Thiamin	10%
Riboflavin	8%
Calcium	8%
Iron	10%

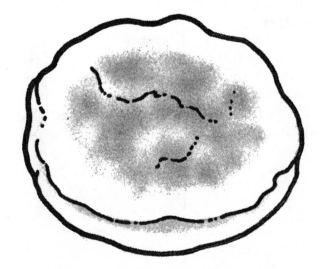

Eggo Homestyle Waffle

Calories	120
Protein	3 grams
Carbohydrates	16 grams
Fat	5 grams

Percentage of U.S. RDA:

Protein	4%
Vitamin A	10%
Thiamin	10%
Riboflavin	10%
Niacin	10%
Calcium	2%
Iron	10%

Downeyflake French Toast (2 slices)

Calories	270
Protein	4 grams
Fat	14 grams

Percentage of U.S. RDA:

Protein	6%
Thiamin	10%
Riboflavin	10%
Niacin	10%
Calcium	8%
Iron	10%

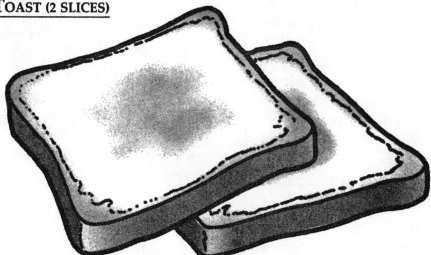

▶

AMERICA THE BAGEL-FUL

To hear Murray Lender tell it, the bagel appeals to the same qualities that have made America great. "The great thing about the American consumer," he has said, "is that they never hesitate to try something new, so long as it tastes great, gives good value, and is nutritionally sound." Words like that make a bagelmaniac proud to be an American!

WONDER ENRICHED HOT DOG ROLL

Calories	100
Protein	3 grams
Carbohydrates	18 grams
Fat	1 gram

Percentage of U.S. RDA:

Protein	4%
Thiamin	10%
Riboflavin	6%
Niacin	6%
Calcium	4%
Iron	6%

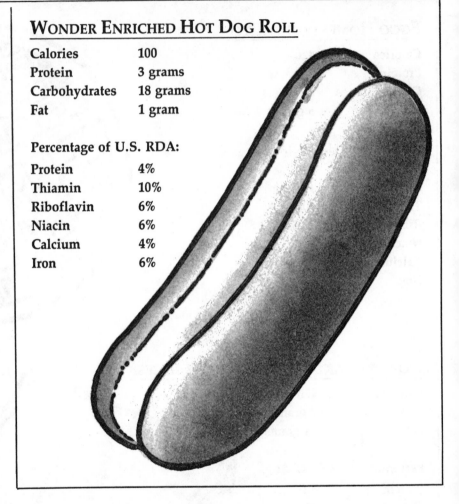

Yes, bagels really are good for you! They're what food analyst Eric Larson defined as ". . . a convenience food that is healthy and doesn't take much effort or preparation."

And the bagel, you'll see, is as adaptable as all emigrants. You can keep it low-cal, make it sinfully and fattening delicious, even use it as a substitute in many of your favorite recipes. Come to think of it, how many other foods that are actually good for your health taste so darned good?

GOOD AND GOOD FOR YOU

If you're a full-fledged bagelmaniac, you don't need to be told that bagels taste delicious. But did you know that they're also good for you? Those redoubtable rings of dough are packed with nutritional value—without the nasty synthetic ingredients and additives of so many other foods.

Bagels are:
- low in calories
- low in sodium
- high in nutrients
- free of cholesterol
- low in saturated fats
- high in protein

That's right! Eating a bagel means never having to say, "I feel guilty."

MAKING YOUR OWN

BAGELS

*East is east and west is west,
home-baked bagels taste the best!*

THE 1-2-3 OF HOME-BAKED BAGELS

Could anything possibly smell much better than the yeasty aroma of bagels hot from the oven? We doubt it. And bagels—any variety your heart desires—aren't especially hard to make. Here are some tips that will help you before you even start:

1. Make a genuine effort when kneading the dough. Remember, in bagel-baking, the

THE POLITICAL BAGEL

Bagels know no party politics: both Democrats and Republicans love 'em! Especially on Saint Patrick's day, when the noshin' of the green is always certain to garner a few lines in the nation's press. As Connecticut Representative Lawrence J. DiNardis put it when he distributed green bagels from Lender's to the House and Senate cafeterias in Washington to celebrate Saint Patrick's Day in 1981, "I am proud to continue the tradition of an Italian Congressman distributing Jewish bagels on an Irish holiday. It is in the finest tradition of our country."

The Irish, of course, have a name for Mr. DiNardis's style of speech. *Blarney*!

development of the gluten is most important if you want to end up with bagels that are chewy but able to be bitten into.

2. Don't leave out or substitute anything else for the gluten flour. You can buy high-gluten flour at any health food store. Look for a flour with 40 percent or higher gluten content.

3. If you use an egg glaze on the bagels, pop them under the broiler for a minute or so before baking (watch them carefully) to get a rich golden crust.

4. Form bagels in either of two ways: by twirling the rounds on your index finger or by rolling strips of dough and then joining the ends in the traditional stirrup shape. Try to

keep your bagels as similar to one another in shape and size as possible, for even baking.

5. The final steps of any bagel recipe—the boiling and baking—should be carried out smoothly, without a hitch, so make sure your work area and necessary utensils and ingredients are ready and close at hand.

WATER BAGELS

Cornmeal
1 (1/4-oz.) package active dry
   yeast (about 1 tablespoon)
3 tablespoons sugar
1 cup warm water (110F/45C)

2 teaspoons salt
2 tablespoons vegetable oil
1/2 cup gluten flour
3-1/2 cups white unbleached
   flour

Lightly dust a baking sheet with cornmeal. In a medium-size bowl, combine yeast and 1 tablespoon of sugar. Pour 1/2 cup of warm water over mixture. Let stand until yeast and sugar have dissolved and yeast is bubbling, then add remaining 1/2 cup of warm water. Add 1 tablespoon of sugar, salt, oil and gluten flour and beat thoroughly. Add white flour, stirring until you have a firm well-mixed dough. If dough reaches firm consistency before all flour has been added, add remaining flour during kneading process. Turn out dough onto a lightly floured board and knead vigorously 10 minutes or until dough is smooth and resilient. Divide dough in 18 equal pieces. Form bagels by rolling pieces of dough in cylinders and fuse ends together. Or form a ball, poke your fingers through to make hole in center and twirl dough until bagel reaches desired size. Place bagels on prepared baking sheet and let rise 20 to 30 minutes in a warm draft-free place. About 10 minutes before bagels have finished rising, bring 3 to 4 quarts of water to a boil in a large stockpot or Dutch oven. Preheat oven to 400F (205C). Lightly dust baking sheet with more cornmeal. Add remaining sugar to boiling water. Drop 3 bagels into boiling water. Bagels should stay on surface or sink and immediately rise. If bagels do not pop right up to surface, they have not risen long enough. Poach each side of each bagel about 2 minutes. When both sides have been poached, remove with a slotted spoon and transfer to prepared baking sheet. Repeat with remaining bagels. Bake in preheated oven about 30 minutes or until perfectly browned. Makes 18 bagels.

VARIATION

To make Egg Bagels, add 2 well-beaten eggs with sugar, salt and oil, then add gluten flour. Before baking, brush with a glaze made with 1 egg white mixed with 1 tablespoon water.

VARIATION

To make Cinnamon-Raisin Bagels, in a custard cup, combine 1 tablespoon sugar with 1 tablespoon ground cinnamon. Roll 1/2 cup raisins in this mixture until well-coated. Add coated raisins during last stages of kneading dough.

POPPY SEED BAGELS

Prepare Water Bagels. After 10 minutes of baking, brush bagels with a glaze made with 1 egg white mixed with 1 tablespoon water. Sprinkle with poppy seeds, then return to oven.

ONION BAGELS

In a small bowl, combine 2 tablespoons dehydrated minced onion and 2 tablespoons water. Let stand 10 minutes. Squeeze all possible water from onions. Glaze as for Poppy Seed Bagels, substituting rehydrated onions for poppy seeds.

GARLIC BAGELS

In a small bowl, combine 2 tablespoons dehydrated garlic flakes and 2 tablespoons water. Let stand 10 minutes. Squeeze all possible water from garlic. Glaze as for Poppy Seed Bagels, substituting rehydrated garlic for poppy seeds.

SESAME SEED BAGELS

Glaze as for Poppy Seed Bagels, substituting sesame seeds for poppy seeds.

SALT BAGELS

Glaze as for Poppy Seed Bagels, substituting coarse sea salt or kosher salt for poppy seeds.

MOTHER'S LITTLE HELPERS

Even *stale* bagels are useful! Since bagel history began, economy-minded mothers have been giving leftover bagels to their toddlers for use as teething rings. So if you've got a little one around, don't trash those bagels after 24 hours: turn them into teething rings. Even your doctor will approve!

WHOLE-WHEAT BAGELS

Cornmeal
1 (1/4-oz.) package active dry yeast (about 1 tablespoon)
1 cup warm water (110F/45C)
2 teaspoons salt
2 eggs, well beaten
1 tablespoon molasses
1/2 cup gluten flour
1-3/4 cups whole-wheat flour
1-1/2 cups white unbleached flour
1/4 cup wheat germ

Lightly dust a baking sheet with cornmeal. In a medium-size bowl, dissolve yeast in 1/2 cup of warm water. Stir in remaining 1/2 cup of warm water. Add salt, eggs, molasses and gluten flour and beat thoroughly. Add whole-wheat and white flours and wheat germ, stirring until you have a firm well-mixed dough. If dough reaches firm consistency before all flour has been added, add remaining flour during kneading process. Turn out dough onto a lightly floured board and knead vigorously 10 minutes or until dough is smooth and resilient. Divide dough in 18 equal pieces. Form bagels by rolling pieces of dough in cylinders and fuse ends together. Or form a ball, poke your fingers through to make hole in center and twirl dough until bagel reaches desired size. Place bagels on prepared baking sheet and let rise 20 to 30 minutes in a warm draft-free place. About 10 minutes before bagels have finished rising, bring 3 to 4 quarts of water to a boil in a large stockpot or Dutch oven. Preheat oven to 400F (205C). Lightly dust baking sheet with more cornmeal. Drop 3 bagels into boiling water. Bagels should stay on surface or sink and immediately rise. If bagels do not pop right up to surface, they have not risen long enough. Poach each side of each bagel about 2 minutes. Remove with a slotted spoon and transfer to a prepared baking sheet. Repeat with remaining bagels. Bake in preheated oven about 30 minutes or until perfectly browned. Makes 18 bagels.

PUMPERNICKEL BAGELS

Cornmeal
1 (1-1/4-oz.) package active dry
  yeast (about 1 tablespoon)
1/2 cup warm water (110F/45C)
1/2 cup warm strong coffee
  (110F/45C)

1 egg, well beaten
1/4 cup molasses
1/2 cup gluten flour
1-3/4 cups whole-wheat flour
1-3/4 cups rye flour

Lightly dust a baking sheet with cornmeal. In a medium-size bowl, dissolve yeast in 1/4 cup of warm water and 1/4 cup of coffee. Stir in remaining 1/4 cup of warm water and 1/4 cup of warm coffee. Add egg, molasses and gluten flour and beat thoroughly. Add whole-wheat and rye flours, stirring until you have a firm well-mixed dough. If dough reaches firm consistency before all flour has been added, add remaining flour during kneading process. Turn out dough onto a lightly floured board and knead vigorously 10 minutes or until dough is smooth and resilient. Divide dough in 18 equal pieces. Form bagels by rolling pieces of dough in cylinders and fuse ends together. Or form a ball, poke your fingers through to make hole in center and twirl dough until bagel reaches desired size. Place bagels on prepared baking sheet and let rise 20 to 30 minutes in a warm draft-free place. About 10 minutes before bagels have finished rising, bring 3 to 4 quarts of water to a boil in a large stockpot or Dutch oven. Preheat oven to 400F (205C). Lightly dust baking sheet with more cornmeal. Drop 3 bagels into boiling water. Bagels should stay on surface or sink and immediately rise. If bagels do not pop right up to surface, they have not risen long enough. Poach each side of each bagel about 2 minutes. When both sides have been poached, remove with a slotted spoon and transfer to prepared baking sheet. Repeat with remaining bagels. Bake in preheated oven about 30 minutes or until perfectly browned. Makes 18 bagels.

THE BAGEL'S BEST SIZE

Look for folks to continue disagreeing over the best size for a bagel long after they've all decided whether the chicken or the egg came first. Because, instead of getting *fewer* bagel sizes from which to choose, we're getting *more*. There's the bite-sized bagelette, perfect for canapes and mini-snacks, and there's the over-size 14-ounce bagel, for parties and institutional use.

LET THEM EAT BAGELS!

While the bagel's origins are mysteriously murky, those of the croissant are part of recorded history. The original crescent roll was a Turkish invention, shaped in honor of the crescent moon on that ancient nation's banner. The Ottomans brought the roll with them when they invaded Austria, from whence it journeyed to France, where it was transformed by skilled *patissiers* into the light and flaky croissant we know today. And which infamous historical figure was responsible for transporting the crescent roll out of her native Austria and into her adopted France? None other than Marie Antoinette. Perhaps if she'd offered the peasants croissants instead of cake. . . .

MATZO BAGELS

1/2 cup vegetable oil
1 cup water
2 cups matzo meal
1 teaspoon salt
1 teaspoon sugar
4 eggs
2 tablespoons shortening
1 tablespoon sesame seeds

Preheat oven to 350F (175C). Grease a baking sheet. In a medium-size saucepan, bring oil and water to a boil. Reduce heat to low. Add matzo meal, salt and sugar all at one time, beating steadily. When mixture pulls away from sides of pan, remove pan from heat. Add eggs, 1 at a time, beating after each egg is added. Beat until mixture is smooth and all ingredients are blended. Coat hands with shortening. Form dough in 10 equal-size balls. Place balls on greased baking sheet, leaving about 2 inches between balls. Using hands, flatten each ball and form a bagel-like hole in center of each. Sprinkle with sesame seeds. Bake in preheated oven 40 to 45 minutes or until "bagels" are lightly browned. Cool on a wire rack.

VARIATION

For a more golden crust, in a custard cup, combine 1 egg white with 1 tablespoon water. Brush Matzo Bagels before baking.

These unleavened "bagels" aren't as chewy as the real thing, but they're tasty and perfect for Passover.

AND YOU DON'T EVEN HAVE TO DIE FIRST!

In the words of that P. T. Barnum of bagelmania Murray Lender, "Biting into a bagel is as close to heaven as you'll ever get."

Montreal Bagels

Which city makes the best bagels in the world? That's a hot topic of debate among bagelmaniacs. Surprisingly, an oft-named bagel mecca is Montreal, Canada. Even some chauvinistic New Yorkers swear that Montreal produces bagels better than anyone else. The Montreal bagel has a distinctive flavor, which it acquires from being bathed in water that is sweetened with malt or honey. It also has a unique slightly-charred outer surface, since the bread is baked in wood ovens. Even if you don't have a wood oven at home, here is a recipe to make the special delight that is known as the Montreal bagel.

1-1/2 cups water (110F/44C)
2 packages active dry
    quick-rising yeast or 1-1/2
    ounces fresh yeast
1 teaspoon sugar
2-1/2 teaspoons salt
1 whole egg
1 egg yolk
1/4 cup vegetable oil
1/2 cup honey
About 5 cups bread flour
3 quarts water
1/3 cup honey or malt syrup
Sesame or poppy seeds

In a large bowl, blend water, yeast, sugar and salt. Stir in whole egg, egg yolk, oil and 1/2 cup honey; mix well. Add 5 cups of flour and mix until dough is too stiff to mix by hand. Transfer to a lightly floured work surface (if using electric mixer, attach dough hook), and knead to form a soft supple dough. Add more flour as needed to prevent dough from getting too sticky. When dough is smooth and elastic, place it in a lightly oiled bowl and cover with plastic wrap or a plastic bag.* Let dough rest about 20 minutes. Punch it down and divide in 18 equal pieces. In a Dutch oven, combine water and 1/3 cup honey or malt syrup and heat to boiling. Cover, reduce heat and allow to simmer while preparing bagels. Line a baking sheet with paper towels. Shape dough pieces in bagels or doughnut-like rings by elongating each piece in an 8- to 10-inch coil that is 3/4-inch thick. Fold ends over each other, pressing with palm of hand and rolling back and forth gently to seal. This locks ends together and must be done properly or bagels will open while

▶

being boiled. Let bagels rest 15 minutes on prepared baking sheet. Preheat oven to 450F (230C). Bring water back to a boil and remove lid. Using a slotted spoon, add 3 bagels to boiling water. As bagels rise to surface, turn bagels over and let them boil 1 minute before removing. Quickly dip bagels in sesame or poppy seeds. Continue boiling bagels in batches of 3 until all have been boiled and seeded. Arrange boiled bagels on a baking sheet and bake on lowest rack of oven about 25 minutes or until medium-brown. Cool; bagels can be placed in a plastic bag, sealed and frozen, if desired. Makes 18 bagels.

*If not using dough immediately, refrigerate after it has been kneaded. Bagel making can be resumed up to a day later. Allow dough to return to room temperature and continue punching it down and dividing it.

Once you've mastered the baking of bagels (and even if you're using "storebought"), you may want to go on to try other Bagel Basics.

Bagel Crumbs

Cut day-old bagels in chunks. In a blender or food processor fitted with a metal blade, process to fine crumbs. These can be substituted for bread crumbs in any recipe.

Bagel Croutons

Preheat oven to 400F (205C). Cut bagels in 1/2-inch cubes. If desired, saute in butter and herbs. Place on a baking sheet. Bake in preheated oven 10 minutes or until lightly browned.

Bagelettes

Follow recipe for Water Bagels, page 56, but divide dough in 30 small bagels. Reduce baking time to 15 to 20 minutes.

Bagel Chips

2 bagels
2 tablespoons butter or margarine, melted, or vegetable oil
Seasoned or herbed salt

Preheat oven to 300F (150C). Slice bagels horizontally in 4 rounds. Place rounds on a baking sheet. Bake, uncovered, in preheated oven about 20 minutes, turning over once during baking. Rounds should be dry and only lightly browned. Brush rounds with 1 tablespoon of melted butter and sprinkle lightly with seasoned salt. Bake 5 minutes, then turn rounds over. Brush with remaining butter and sprinkle with more seasoned salt. Bake 5 minutes more. Makes 8 bagel chips.

Though not as thin as commerically made bagel chips, these are every bit as delicious—and fresh as you make them! We'd advise not to keep these any longer than three days or so.

BIALYS

The bialy is the bagel's cousin, often known as a "water roll." The bialy isn't boiled first and has no hole. It is usually topped with onions.

Cornmeal
2 tablespoons water
2 tablespoons minced dehydrated onions
2 teaspoons vegetable oil
1 (1/4-oz.) package active dry yeast (about 1 tablespoon)

2 tablespoons sugar
1 cup warm water (110F/45C)
2 teaspoons salt
2 tablespoons vegetable oil
1/2 cup gluten flour
3-1/2 cups white unbleached flour

Lightly dust a baking sheet with cornmeal. In a small bowl, combine water and onions. Let stand until onions are rehydrated, about 10 minutes. Squeeze water from onions and combine with oil. Set aside. In a medium-size bowl, combine yeast and 1 tablespoon of sugar. Pour 1/2 cup of warm water over mixture. Let stand until yeast and sugar have dissolved and yeast is bubbling, then add remaining 1/2 cup of warm water. Add remaining 1 tablespoon of sugar, salt, oil and gluten flour and beat thoroughly. Add white flour, stirring until you have a firm well-mixed dough. If dough reaches firm consistency before all flour has been added, add remaining flour during kneading process. Turn out dough onto a lightly floured board and knead vigorously 10 minutes or until dough is smooth and resilient. Divide dough in 18 equal pieces. Form bialys by rolling each piece of dough in a ball. Flatten until it resembles a burger bun, somewhat fatter in center. Using a spoon or your fingers, make an indentation in center of each dough patty (as if making a hole without going all way through). Place bialys on prepared baking sheet. Fill bialy holes with onions. Let rise 20 to 30 minutes in a warm draft-free place. Preheat oven to 400F (205C). Bake in preheated oven about 30 minutes or until perfectly browned. Makes 18 bialys.

THE
WELL-
DRESSED
BAGEL

No other bread can "top" the bagel,
but bagel toppings can make
a good thing even better!

THE A TO Z OF BAGEL TOPPINGS

The only comestible better than a bagel might be a bagel after it's been topped or filled! You can let your imagination—and your stomach—run wild when dressing up bagels. The opportunities are endless, and everyone has his or her own favorite bagel combo, which range from the Occidentally unappetizing Japanese delight of lox and cream cheese on cinnamon-raisin to a friend's favorite nosh of ketchup and pickle slices on a plain bagel (and, no, there are no ingredients missing in that recipe). You need never be stumped, because bagels can be topped from A to Z!

BAGEL ALPHABET

- *A*nchovy paste on ONION
- Sliced *b*anana and honey on CINNAMON-RAISIN
- *C*orned beef and Swiss on POPPY SEED
- Chopped *d*ates and cream cheese on PLAIN
- *E*gg salad and olives on RYE
- Fried *f*ish fillet and tartar sauce on EGG
- Hot *g*oat cheese and romaine on SESAME SEED
- Roast beef with *h*orseradish on PUMPERNICKEL
- *I*ce cream with chocolate sauce on CINNAMON-RAISIN
- Guava *j*elly and cream cheese on PLAIN
- Chocolate *k*isses baked with marshmallow fluff on SESAME SEED
- *L*ox on PUMPERNICKEL
- Sliced chicken and *m*ango chutney on POPPY SEED
- *N*ectarine slices and deviled ham on PLAIN
- Fried *o*nions and bacon on ONION
- Liver *p*ate and gherkins on WHOLE WHEAT
- *Q*uince preserves and sour cream on SESAME SEED
- *R*elish and lunch meat on GARLIC
- *S*alami and mustard on PUMPERNICKEL
- *T*omato, lettuce and mayonnaise on PLAIN
- '*U*mmas and cucumbers on POPPY SEED (okay, so we cheated)
- Sliced *v*eal and tomato sauce on ONION
- Cold *w*urst and sauerkraut on RYE
- *X*tra butter!
- *Y*esterday's meal is tomorrow's bagel topping!
- It's so E-*Z* to dress up a bagel!

A Bagel Is a Bagel Is a Bagel...

It's been mispronounced as a "bockle" or a "baggle." Aside from mispronunciations, the bagel has been called some downright outrageous things in its time, including:

crocodile's teething ring
Israeli sportscar tire
Brooklyn jawbreaker
water doughnut
Jewish English muffin
mouse's life preserver
unsweetened doughnut with rigor mortis

To bagelmaniacs, a bagel by any other name is still a bagel, the food world's most desirable wheel of flavor!

The Dagwood Bagel

As every bagel maven knows from experimentation, almost everything goes better with a bagel. If you're a late-night nosher with a craving for crazy combinations à la Bumstead, you'll find the Dagwood Bagel just what the Sandman (and the sandwichman) ordered!

You don't have to be a great cook to put together your own unique version of the Dagwood Bagel. It's simple as can be: just take two halves from Column A, add a minimum of two ingredients from Column B, dress with at least one item from Column C, then crown with as many bagel boosters from Column D as you like! Serve open-faced (or close it if you can!) and you definitely won't wake up hungry an hour later!

A	B	C	D
Plain bagel	Roast beef	Lettuce	Mayonnaise
Onion bagel	Boiled ham	Tomato	Mustard
Egg bagel	Tuna salad	Onion	Ketchup
Sesame bagel	Turkey	Swiss cheese	Relish
Poppy bagel	Deviled ham	Cheddar Cheese	Sesame seeds
Garlic bagel	Tongue	Monterey Jack	Olive oil
Rye bagel	Salami	Pimiento	Vinegar
Pumpernickel	Capiccola	Anchovies	Corn relish
	Bologna	Cream cheese	Pickles
	Nova or lox	Sour cream	Cucumber slices
	Corned beef	Sauerkraut	Oregano
	Pastrami	Hot peppers	Bacon bits
	Egg salad	Sweet peppers	Duck sauce
	Roast pork	Coleslaw	Hot sauce
	Sloppy Joe	Bean sprouts	Cranberry relish
	Lunch meat	Olives	Russian dressing

As you might have guessed, the bigger the bagel, the better the Dagwood. We recommend making this man-size sandwich with bagels weighing three ounces or more. Or, for a party, why not bake your own super-size bagel and let guests cut off chunks?

MIX 'N' MATCH TOPPINGS

Right now, you might be saying, "I know everything tastes better on a bagel, but I could never eat all *that*!" Don't des-

pair. A bagel never needs the contents of an entire delicatessen heaped upon it to tempt your taste. Certain foods naturally lend themselves to the making of bagelwiches, and

we've come up with some mix 'n' match suggestions that should soothe any cravings you may have. The choice of bagel flavor is entirely up to you.

▶

Peanut butter with

- Sliced banana
- Bacon and mayonnaise
- Honey
- Fruit preserves
- Chutney
- Toasted coconut
- Raisins
- Marshmallow fluff
- Fresh figs

Sour cream with

- Anchovies
- Smoked Oysters
- Bananas and brown sugar
- Roast peppers
- Minced onions
- Herring
- Beef and horseradish
- Cucumber slices
- Marinated mushrooms

Cream cheese with

- Ripe olives, Nova or lox
- Red caviar
- Chutney and raisins
- Dates and walnuts
- Chopped chives
- Pecans and honey
- Currant jelly
- Mandarin orange segments

SOMEDAY WE'LL ALL BE SINGING,

"I Left My Lox In San Francisco"

Is the world ready for the sourdough bagel? Its day may come...sooner than some of us would wish. Kraft, now the owner of Lender's, recently signed a licensing agreement with San Francisco French Bread Company, giving Kraft permission to market a line of sourdough French bread and other sourdough products. And a top executive at Kraft was soon admitting that there were "certainly opportunities for the two pieces of business [sourdough and bagel] to benefit each other." So the Golden Gate Bagel may soon be on the way!

Egg salad with

- Green olives
- Bacon bits
- Pimientos
- Capers
- Alfalfa sprouts
- Pickled onions
- Green pepper
- Sun-dried tomatoes
- Sunflower seeds

BAGEL SPREAD DELIGHTS

Perhaps you have simpler tastes and like your bagels less hearty. Then one of our special bagel butters is for you! Bagel butters can be made ahead of time and stored in the refrigerator to be accessible at a moment's craving. Spread them on the bagel of your choice, sliced, then toast or warm.

Bagel butters can be whipped up from scratch in minutes, using the metal blade of a food processor or by creaming in the ingredients by hand with the butter at room temperature.

▶

BAGEL BUTTERS

Bagel butters and bagel blends are delicious. You'll find it easy and challenging to come up with your own. Unfortunately for those striving to decrease their saturated fat intake, butters lose something if made with margarine. However, we've had good results making them with butter/corn oil spreads now available in the markets.

CURRY RAISIN BUTTER

Cream 1 stick sweet butter with 1/4 cup chopped chutney, 3 tablespoons raisins and 1/2 teaspoon curry powder.

LEMON BUTTER

Cream 1 stick sweet butter with 1/3 cup lemon marmalade (or lemon curd), 1 teaspoon grated lemon peel, 1 teaspoon powdered sugar and 1 teaspoon fresh lemon juice.

CINNAMON BUTTER

Cream 1 stick sweet butter with 1 teaspoon ground cinnamon, 1 teaspoon powdered sugar and 1/4 teaspoon ground nutmeg.

STRAWBERRY BUTTER

Cream 1 stick sweet butter with 1/2 cup fresh strawberries (puree strawberries first if mixing by hand), 2 tablespoons strawberry preserves, 1 teaspoon powdered sugar and 1/4 teaspoon fresh lemon juice.

RUM BUTTER

Cream 1 stick sweet butter with 2 tablespoons dark rum, 1 teaspoon powdered sugar and 1/4 teaspoon ground cinnamon.

HERB BUTTER

For cold meat, poultry and fish bagelwiches, cream 1 stick sweet or lightly salted butter with approximately 1 tablespoon of any of the following fresh herbs: basil, parsley, tarragon, sage, oregano or thyme.

BAGEL BLENDS

Want something a little more filling than a bagel butter but not as heavy as a whole bagelwich? Try one of our lip smacking bagel blends.

APPLE BUTTER BAGEL BLEND

Cream 1 (8-oz.) package cream cheese with 1/2 cup apple butter and 1/2 teaspoon powdered sugar.

PRUNE BUTTER BAGEL BLEND

Cream 1 (8-oz.) package cream cheese, 1/2 cup lekvar (available wherever Eastern European foodstuffs are sold) and 1/2 teaspoon powdered sugar.

CHOCOLATE BAGEL BLEND

Cream 1 (8-oz.) package cream cheese, 2 (1-oz.) squares baking chocolate, melted (make that 3 (1-oz.) squares for chocoholic bagelmaniacs), 1 teaspoon powdered sugar and, if desired, 1/2 teaspoon creme de cocoa.

HOT STUFF BAGEL BLEND

Cream 1 (8-oz.) package cream cheese, 2 tablespoons sweet pickle relish and 1/4 teaspoon hot-pepper sauce

GRASSHOPPER BAGEL BLEND

Cream 1 (8-oz.) package cream cheese, 1/2 teaspoon light creme de cocoa and 1/2 teaspoon green creme de menthe.

RASPBERRY BAGEL BLEND

Cream 1 (8-oz.) package cream cheese, 3 tablespoons thawed frozen raspberries and 1/2 teaspoon Chambord.

CHERRY BAGEL BLEND

Cream 1 (8-oz.) package cream cheese, 1/4 cup cherry preserves and 1/2 teaspoon kirsch.

THE "PERFECT MARRIAGE"

No tyro when it comes to creating good publicity schemes in his commitment to "bagelize" America, Murray outdid himself when his company was acquired by Kraft in 1984.

Guests, including 450 food brokers, were invited to celebrate the wedding of the century—between the eight-foot bride (Philadelphia Cream Cheese) and groom (the bagel). Actually the bride topped eight feet because the model wearing the silver cream cheese package costume also wore high heels! Attendants included giant-size versions of Kraft Singles, Velveeta, Parkay, and a variety of Lender's Bagels flavors. The couple honeymooned at an undisclosed location. A toaster, maybe?

THE HARD-WORKING BAGELS

Good as bagels are to eat, they can also fulfill a host of
other uses when they're too stale to eat. Simply shellac
them and you've got:

- A pencil holder (glue three bagels together vertically)
- Nosher's napkin rings
- A spare tire for a toy car
- Unusual earrings
- A ponytail holder
- A doorstop

- Coasters (use bagel halves)
- A trivet (join four bagels together in a square)
- A pomander (stick with cloves)
- Refrigerator decor (glue on magnets)
- A paperweight
- A hockey puck

BIRTH OF THE BAGELHEAD

For her son's Bar Mitzvah, Murray Lender's wife wanted a cute party favor. An artist friend came up with the idea of painting faces on bagelettes to make Bagelheads, and soon Lender's was selling bagel jewelry as well as bagels! You can make your own Bagelheads with some leftover bagels and paints (and shellac for preserving). A Lender family favorite is the "Lepre-cohen," a green bagel with a leprechaun's features for St. Patrick's Day. And the true bagelmaniac can follow the Lenders' lead and use preserved bagelettes as shade pulls at home!

SECTION
5

RECIPES

---

*From appetizers to desserts,
46 ways to cook with bagels.*

NOT-SO-FRENCH TOAST

A real change of pace. French toast lovers will go for this one.

4 eggs
1/3 cup milk
1/2 teaspoon vanilla extract
4 cinnamon-raisin bagels, sliced
1 tablespoon butter
Ground cinnamon
Ground nutmeg

RAISIN-PECAN SYRUP:

1 cup pancake or maple
  syrup
1/4 cup raisins
2 tablespoons chopped
  pecans

Prepare Raisin-Pecan Syrup; set aside. In a small bowl, beat eggs, milk and vanilla. Pierce each bagel half several times. Pour egg mixture into a flat-bottomed glass baking dish. Soak bagel halves about 1 hour, turning frequently to make sure they are saturated. Melt butter in a large skillet or on griddle. Drain bagels; place, sliced-side down, in skillet. Cook until browned; turn and cook on other side. Sprinkle with cinnamon and nutmeg. Serve topped with Raisin-Pecan Syrup. (Serves 4)

RAISIN-PECAN SYRUP:

Combine all ingredients in a small saucepan. Simmer 15 minutes. Serve warm.

TOP O' THE MORNING

What a way to greet the day!

2 onion bagels, sliced
4 eggs
4 tablespoons milk
1/4 pound Nova Scotia
  salmon, chopped

Pepper to taste
1 tablespoon butter
1/4 pound cream cheese

Toast bagels. In a small bowl, beat eggs and milk. Add salmon and pepper. Melt butter in a medium-size skillet and quickly scramble egg mixture until cooked but creamy. Spread bagel halves with cream cheese and top with eggs. (Serves 2)

BAGELKUCHEN

Coffee Cake—with a twist. This makes a great breakfast or snack.

2 tablespoons sugar
1 tablespoon all-purpose flour
1 tablespoon butter, softened

1 plain bagel, sliced
Ground cinnamon
Ground nutmeg

On a pastry board, cut sugar and flour into butter until mixture forms crumbs. Scoop out both bagel halves just enough to make a slight hollow in each. Fill hollows with sugar crumbs. Sprinkle with cinnamon and nutmeg. Toast kuchen in a toaster oven, or bake in a 375F (190C) oven about 7 to 10 minutes or until heated through. (Serves 1)

BAGELS MORNAY

A breakfast fancy enough for a party brunch.

4 slices Canadian bacon
2 egg bagels, sliced
1 tablespoon white vinegar
4 eggs
1 cup hot Cheese Sauce, Turkey Divan Bagels, page 104

In a skillet, saute bacon until lightly browned. Toast bagels. Place bacon slices on bagel halves. Fill a medium-size saucepan half full of water and add vinegar. Bring water to a boil. Poach eggs in boiling water. Carefully place poached eggs on bacon. Top with hot Cheese Sauce. (Serves 4)

BAGEL McBAGEL

Try this recipe for brunch with spicy Bloody Marys.

1/4 cup chopped green
   pepper
1/4 cup chopped onion
2 tablespoons vegetable oil
1 (8-oz.) can stewed
   tomatoes
2 (3-1/2-oz.) cans green
   chiles, chopped
2 plain bagels, sliced
4 eggs
2 tablespoons butter

In a small skillet, saute green pepper and onion in oil until wilted. In a small saucepan, combine green pepper and onion mixture with tomatoes. Stir in chiles and bring to a boil. Toast bagels. In a medium skillet, fry eggs in butter. Put 2 bagel halves side by side on each of 2 plates. Top each half with a fried egg. Spoon sauce over egg. (Serves 2)

TIJUANA TOPPING

This guacamole spread is especially tasty served with bagel chips and margaritas.

1 ripe avocado, chopped
1 tomato, chopped, peeled
1/2 small onion, chopped
3 tablespoons lime juice
1/2 green chile, chopped
Hot-pepper sauce to taste
Bagel chips

Place avocado, tomato, onion, lime juice, green chile and hot-pepper sauce in a blender and blend at low speed. Spoon into a small serving bowl. Serve with a platter of bagel chips. (Makes 1-1/2 cups)

THE GODFATHER BAGEL

You don't have to be a member of the mob to appreciate hot bread redolent of garlic. Here's a Mulberry Street-style accompaniment for pasta dishes, or for just plain snacking.

1/2 cup butter, softened
4 plain bagels, sliced
2 garlic cloves, minced
2 tablespoons fresh parsley, finely chopped

Preheat oven to 350F (175C). Liberally spread butter on bagel halves. In a custard cup, combine garlic and parsley; sprinkle on bagel halves. Put bagel halves together and wrap each loosely in foil. Bake in preheated oven 10 to 15 minutes. (Serves 4)

SESAME SNACK MIX

These bite-sized morsels were made for Super Bowl Sundays.

2 cups bite-sized cereal squares
3/4 cup mini-pretzels or pretzel thins
1 cup Sesame Bagel "Buttons"
1/2 cup roasted peanuts
1/4 cup butter, melted
2 tablespoons Worcestershire sauce
Dash chili powder
Dash garlic powder
Dash onion salt

SESAME BAGEL "BUTTONS":

1 to 2 sesame bagels

Preheat oven to 350F (175C). Combine cereal, pretzels, Sesame Bagel "Buttons" and peanuts in a shallow rectangular baking dish. In a small bowl, combine butter and remaining ingredients. Pour butter mixture over dry mixture and toss lightly until coated. Bake in preheated oven 15 to 20 minutes, stirring every 5 minutes. Spread mix on foil to cool. (Makes 4-1/4 cups)

SESAME BAGEL "BUTTONS":

Cut bagel in strips, then cut each strip in small squares.

BENGALI BAGEL DIP

Exotic yet easy to make, this dip is based on the classic Indian raita.

1 large cucumber
Salt
1/2 clove garlic, crushed
1/4 teaspoon chopped fresh
  ginger

1/2 cup plain yogurt
2 tablespoons lemon juice
Dash cumin
Dash salt
Bagel chips

Peel cucumber and slice thinly. Place slices in a shallow bowl and sprinkle lightly with salt; refrigerate 1 hour. In a small bowl, combine garlic, ginger, yogurt, lemon juice, cumin and salt. Refrigerate until chilled. To serve, drain cucumbers and combine with yogurt mixture. Serve with bagel chips for dipping. (Makes about 1 cup)

MIDDLE EASTERN HUMMUS DIP

This vegetarian delight is as tasty as it is nutritious.

1 small eggplant
Salt
1/2 cup olive oil
1 clove garlic, mashed
1/4 cup plain yogurt
2 tablespoons fresh
  parsley, chopped finely
Garlic bagel chips

Cover a plate with a paper towel. Peel eggplant and slice thinly. Stack eggplant on paper towel, sprinkling each slice with salt. Cover stack with a paper towel, a second plate and a weight, such as a heavy book. Let eggplant stand at least 1/2 hour. Drain, pressing to remove all of liquid. Heat olive oil in a large skillet. Saute eggplant and garlic until lightly browned on both sides. Drain on paper towels. Puree eggplant, yogurt and parsley in a blender. Serve with bagel chips. (Makes 2 cups)

BLACK TIE BAGEL

1 (8-oz.) package cream
   cheese
1/4 cup milk
1 tablespoon chopped
   pecans
10 to 12 bagelettes, sliced
1 tablespoon lemon juice
1 (4-oz.) jar lumpfish
   caviar
20 to 24 thin pimiento
   strips, if desired

*In a small bowl, blend cream
cheese, milk and pecans.
Lightly toast bagelettes;
spread with cream-cheese
mixture. Drizzle lemon juice
over caviar; place a dollop
on each bagelette half. If desired, twist pimiento strips
into bows; garnish hors
d'oeuvres with pimiento
bows. (Makes 20 to 24 hors
d'oeuvres)*

---

*You may have to
double this recipe for
a crowd—it's hard to
stop after eating just
one.*

BAGELS TARTARE

*Dress up any evening
with these elegant
little hors d'oeuvres.*

1 pound very lean ground sirloin
1 egg yolk
1/2 cup chili sauce or catsup
1/2 small onion, finely chopped
2 tablespoons capers, chopped, drained
1 tablespoon Worchestershire sauce
Salt to taste
Freshly ground pepper to taste
6 to 8 bagelettes, sliced
1 tablespoon butter
Additional capers, if desired

In a medium-size bowl, combine sirloin, egg yolk, chili sauce, onion, capers, Worchestershire sauce, salt and pepper. Form in 12 to 16 small balls, then flatten slightly. Lightly toast bagelettes. Spread with butter and top with tartare patties. Garnish with capers, if desired. (Makes 12 to 16 hors d'oeuvres)

BLT BAGEL

A variation on an old deli favorite, bagels and BLT's have a crunchy taste appeal.

1 plain bagel, sliced
2 strips bacon
Mayonnaise
1/2 tomato, sliced
Several leaves iceberg lettuce
Salt to taste
Pepper to taste

Lightly toast bagel. In a small skillet, fry bacon until crisp. Break each strip of bacon in half. Spread each bagel half with mayonnaise. Top 1 bagel half with bacon, tomato and lettuce. Season with salt and pepper. Top with remaining bagel half. Secure with wooden picks, if desired. (Serves 1)

THE KENNETT SQUARE BAGEL BOAT

From Kennett Square, Pennsylvania—the mushroom capital of America—come these bagel boats, an ideal lunch entree or dinner starter.

2 onion bagels, sliced
1/4 pound mushrooms, chopped
6 slices bacon, chopped
1/2 small onion, chopped
1 cup sour cream
2 teaspoons butter

Preheat oven to 350F (175C). Lightly butter a medium-size baking pan. Scoop out centers of bagel halves. Crumble removed bagel centers. In a medium-size skillet, saute mushrooms, bacon and onion until bacon is done but not too crisp. Drain on paper towels. In a small bowl, combine bacon mixture and sour cream. Fill bagel shells with sour cream mixture, then top with bagel crumbs. Dot with butter and place in buttered pan. Bake in preheated oven 15 to 20 minutes. (Serves 2)

THE CAPE CODDER

Keep this spread on hand for middle-of-the-night snacking.

1 (6-1/2-oz.) can chopped clams
1 (8-oz.) package cream cheese
1/3 cup sour cream
1 teaspoon chopped fresh parsley
3 onion bagels, sliced
Paprika

In a small bowl, combine clams, cream cheese, sour cream and parsley. Chill well. Toast bagels; spread with cream-cheese mixture. Sprinkle with paprika. (Serves 3)

TEXAS CHILI BAGELS

*This chuckwagon
classic will warm up
the coldest winter
night.*

**1 medium-size onion, chopped
1 clove garlic, minced
1 green bell pepper, chopped
2 tablespoons vegetable oil
1 pound ground or chopped beef
1 (35-oz.) can tomatoes, peeled, seeded
2 cups water
1 cup tomato juice
1/2 green chili pepper, finely chopped
2 to 4 tablespoons chili powder or to taste
1/2 teaspoon cumin
1 (16-oz.) can kidney beans, drained
4 plain or onion bagels
1/2 pound Cheddar cheese, shredded**

In a large skillet, saute onion, garlic and bell pepper in oil;
add meat. Cook until meat is brown; drain. In a Dutch oven,
combine meat mixture, tomatoes, water, tomato juice, chili
pepper, chili powder and cumin. Bring mixture to a boil,
stirring constantly. Reduce heat, simmer, uncovered, 1-1/2
hours or until chili has thickened. Add kidney beans. Cook
10 minutes more. Slice bagels. Serve chili over bagels with
cheese on side. (Serves 4)

NORTHWEST TERRITORY BAGELS

An homage to the Pacific Northwest, this recipe features delicate sesame bagels with an equally delicate salmon mousse.

1/2 pound smoked salmon
1 (8-oz.) package cream cheese
1/4 cup chopped onion
2 tablespoons lemon juice
2 sesame bagels, sliced
40 small Spanish capers

In a blender or food processor fitted with the steel knife, blend salmon, cream cheese, onion and lemon juice. Spoon into a bowl and chill. Lightly toast bagel halves. Spread with mousse. Top each bagel half with 10 capers. (Serves 2)

THE WILLIAMSBURG BAGEL

Like having a lunch entree and dessert in one, this delivers old-time tastiness.

2 tablespoons peach or apricot preserves
1 teaspoon currant jelly
1 teaspoon orange marmalade
1 cinnamon-raisin bagel, sliced
1 thick slice Virginia ham
1 canned or fresh peach half, cut in half

Preheat oven to 350F (175C). In a custard cup, mix preserves, jelly and marmalade. Lightly toast bagel. Spread each bagel half with 1/4 of jam mixture. Place 1 bagel half in a small baking dish. Top with ham, peach slices, remaining jam mixture, and remaining bagel half. Bake in preheated oven 10 to 15 minutes or until heated through. (Serves 1)

MIAMI NICE BAGELS

4 ounces cream cheese
1 heaping teaspoon
  superfine sugar
1 tablespoon Grand
  Marnier
1 teaspoon grated
  orange peel
4 egg bagels

In a blender, process cream cheese, sugar, Grand Marnier and orange peel at low setting until well-blended. Chill, covered, at least 2 hours. Bring to room temperature. Slice and toast bagels. Spread bagels with cream cheese mixture. (Serves 4)

VARIATION

KEY LIME BAGELS: Substitute Midori for Grand Marnier and grated lime peel for orange peel.

A shot of after dinner liqueur gives this bagel treat added pizzazz.

We give the Cubano sandwich a few new twists!

THE CUBAN REUBEN

1 (3-inch) kielbasa, cut in
   half lengthwise
1 rye bagel, sliced
Polish mustard
1/3 cup sauerkraut
1 slice Swiss cheese

Preheat oven to 350F (175C). In a small skillet, saute kielbasa until browned. Spread 1 bagel half with mustard. Place kielbasa on mustard, then add sauerkraut. Top with cheese. Bake in preheated oven until cheese is melted. To serve, top with remaining bagel half. (Serves 1)

Good enough to make from scratch, these Middle Eastern marvels can also be made from leftovers.

LEBANESE LAMB BAGELS

1/2 small eggplant
Salt
1/2 cup olive oil
1 pound lean ground lamb

1/4 cup chopped fresh parsley
Ground cinnamon to taste
Pepper to taste
4 sesame bagels, sliced

Cut unpeeled eggplant in 4 (3/4-inch-thick) slices. Sprinkle with salt and drain on paper towels 1/2 hour. Place eggplant in a shallow dish and add olive oil. Marinate eggplant 1/2 hour. Remove eggplant from oil and blot with paper towels. In a blender or with a mortar and pestle, mash lamb and parsley until consistency is smooth. Form in burger-size patties. Sprinkle with cinnamon and pepper. Brush lamb patties with leftover oil. Broil patties and eggplant slices until meat is well-browned and eggplant is done. Lightly toast bagel halves. Place 1 eggplant slice on each of 4 bagel halves. Top with lamb patties and sprinkle with cinnamon. Top with remaining bagel halves. (Serves 4)

RED SQUARE BAGEL

From Russia, home of the bubliki, *comes this stick-to-the ribs main course!*

1 pound lean round beefsteak or flank steak
2 tablespoons butter or margarine
2 teaspoons all-purpose flour
1/2 cup beef broth
1/2 onion, thinly sliced
6 bagelettes, sliced
1/2 cup sour cream, room temperature

Slice steak in narrow (1/2-inch-thick) strips; chill. In a small saucepan, melt 1 tablespoon of butter. Stir in flour until well-blended. In a small saucepan, heat beef broth to boiling. Add to flour mixture, stirring constantly until completely blended. In a small skillet, saute steak and onion in remaining 1 tablespoon of butter about 7 to 10 minutes or until steak is no longer pink. Toast bagelettes. Place on a serving platter, sliced-sides up. Add sour cream to sauce.
Cook over high heat just until hot, stirring constantly. Spoon meat and onions over bagelettes. Top with sauce. (Serves 4)

ROMAN SPEDINI BAGELS

These mouth-watering appetizers need only a salad on the side to star at an intimate luncheon.

6 onion bagels, sliced
3/4 cup olive oil
4 tablespoons butter
6 anchovy fillets, chopped
1 tablespoon capers, chopped
1 clove garlic, minced
1/2 cup dry white wine
12 slices mozzarella cheese

Cut a thin slice off bottom of each bagel half so halves have flat bottoms. Reserve thin slices for another use. In a large skillet or on a griddle, heat olive oil. Fry bagel halves until browned on both sides. Drain on paper towels. To make sauce, heat butter in a small saucepan. Add anchovies, capers and garlic. Cook over medium heat 2 minutes, stirring constantly. Increase heat slightly. Cook 5 minutes more, stirring constantly. Stir in wine. Top each bagel half with a slice of cheese. Broil until cheese begins to brown. Remove to a serving platter and cover with sauce. (Serves 6)

BAGEL à la RUSSE

This elegant appetizer also makes a great midnight supper when accompanied by a flute of champagne or lemon-flavored iced vodka.

1 onion bagel half
2 tablespoons sour cream
1 tablespoon lumpfish caviar
1 egg, hardboiled
1 lemon wedge

Slice bagel half in thirds horizonally. Lightly toast bagel slices. Stack with biggest slice on bottom and smallest on top, shiny side up. Liberally spread sour cream between layers. Fill bagel hole with caviar. Separate yolk from white of hardboiled egg; finely chop each. Arrange yolk and white on either side of bagel stack. Serve with lemon. (Serves 1)

OLDE ENGLISH HIGH TEA BAGEL

1/2 pound sharp Cheddar cheese, shredded
1/2 teaspoon dry mustard
Dash Worchestershire sauce
Dash cayenne pepper
1/2 cup beer or ale
1 rye or pumpernickel bagel, sliced
1 plain bagel, sliced
1 tomato, cut in 4 slices

To make sauce, in a small saucepan, combine cheese, mustard, Worchestershire sauce and cayenne pepper. Cook over low heat. Gradually add beer, stirring constantly until all cheese has melted and rarebit is smooth and fully blended. Toast bagels. Place 1 plain bagel half and 1 rye bagel half on each of 2 plates. Top each bagel half with a tomato slice, then cover with sauce. (Serves 2)

In Britain, the term "cream tea" means one with sweets and tiny sandwiches. The "high tea" is heartier and features a hot dish. This variation on the classic Welsh rarebit will drive away the chill of a winter's day.

BAGELS MEXICANO

Tex-Mex meets bagelmania in spicy, succulent style!

1/2 pound ground beef
1/2 cup water
2 plain bagels, sliced
1/2 cup refried beans
2 cups shredded lettuce
2 tomatoes, chopped
1 small onion, chopped
1/2 pound Cheddar cheese, shredded
1/2 cup mayonnaise
1/4 cup salsa or prepared taco sauce

In a small saucepan, combine beef and water. Bring to a boil. Decrease heat to simmer. Cook until meat is no longer pink, breaking up beef with a wooden spoon. Drain in colander. Toast bagels. Put 2 halves on each of 2 plates, sliced-sides up. Layer with beef, beans, lettuce, tomatoes, onions and cheese. In a small bowl, combine mayonnaise and salsa. Spoon over "bageladas." (Serves 2)

INDONESIAN RIFSTAFEL BAGEL

Here's a sweet yet succulent sandwich treat that turns yesterday's beef into today's pièce de résistance.

**3 tablespoons crunchy
  peanut butter**
1/2 cup water
1 tablespoon brown sugar
1 tablespoon dark soy sauce
1/4 teaspoon garlic salt
Squeeze lemon juice
1 cinnamon-raisin bagel, sliced
3 to 4 slices cooked beef

In a small saucepan, heat peanut butter and water over low heat, stirring constantly until fully blended. Remove from heat and add brown sugar, soy sauce, garlic salt and lemon juice, thinning with more water if necessary. Toast bagel. Place bagel halves on a serving plate. Cover bagel halves with beef and top with peanut sauce. (Serves 1)

BOMBAY BAGEL

Here's a treat that can perk up a brown-bag lunch. And you can cut calories by using reduced-calorie mayonnaise.

1 egg, hard-boiled
1 tablespoon mayonnaise
1/4 teaspoon curry powder
1 egg bagel, sliced
1 tablespoon mango
   chutney, finely chopped

Chop egg. In a small bowl, mash egg with a fork until fine. Blend in mayonnaise and curry powder. Spread mixture on 1 bagel half. Spread remaining bagel half with chutney. Serve open or closed. (Serves 1)

DOWN-HOME CHICKEN HASH BAGELS

Bring Dixie to your dining room by serving these with collard greens or black-eyed peas.

2 tablespoons butter
1/4 cup finely chopped onion
3 tablespoons all-purpose flour
1-1/2 cups chicken broth
2 cups half and half
1/2 cup chopped apple
1/2 cup chopped walnuts
2 cups cubed cooked chicken
4 poppy-seed bagels, sliced
Freshly ground pepper to taste

In a medium-size skillet, melt butter and saute onion until golden. Remove from heat and add flour, stirring until smooth. Return pan to heat and gradually add chicken broth, stirring constantly until sauce thickens. Add half and half, stirring constantly until sauce rethickens. Stir in apple, walnuts and chicken. Cook 5 minutes or until all ingredients are piping hot. Toast bagels and slice in thin strips. Place bagel strips on a platter. Pour hash over bagels and season with pepper. (Serves 4 to 6)

TURKEY DIVAN BAGELS

An old standby gets new life with the simple addition of a bagel.

2 plain bagels, sliced
1 (10-oz.) package frozen broccoli, thawed
8 slices cooked turkey

CHEESE SAUCE:

2 tablespoons butter
2 tablespoons all-purpose flour
1 cup milk
2/3 cup shredded Cheddar cheese
1/4 teaspoon dry mustard
Dash cayenne pepper

Prepare Cheese Sauce; set aside. Preheat oven to 350F (175C). Butter a medium-size shallow baking dish. Place bagel halves in buttered dish. Cover with broccoli spears, then turkey. Top with Cheese Sauce. Bake in preheated oven 15 to 20 minutes or until heated through. (Serves 4)

CHEESE SAUCE:

Melt butter in a small saucepan. Stir in flour until blended. Gradually add milk, stirring constantly until sauce is smooth and hot. Reduce heat and gradually add cheese, stirring constantly until sauce is smooth and all cheese has melted. Stir in mustard and cayenne. (Makes 1-1/4 cups)

BAGELS à la KING

*Treat leftovers royally
with this bagelicious
luncheon or dinner
entree.*

5 tablespoons butter
1/2 cup mushrooms, sliced
1/4 cup chopped red bell
   pepper
4 tablespoons flour
1 cup chicken broth
1 cup half and half
1 cup cubed cooked
   chicken, turkey or ham
1 egg yolk
2 egg bagels, sliced
1 tablespoon dry sherry

In a small skillet, melt 2 tablespoons of butter. Saute mushrooms and bell pepper. In a small saucepan, melt remaining 3 tablespoons of butter. Gradually stir in flour until blended. Add chicken broth and half and half, a little at a time, stirring gently. Bring to a boil. Stir in mushroom mixture and meat. Reduce heat. In a small bowl, combine egg yolk and a small amount of sauce. Pour egg back into sauce, stirring constantly until sauce has thickened. Toast bagels and put 2 bagel halves on each of 2 plates. Stir sherry into sauce; pour sauce over bagel halves. (Serves 2)

BAGELS à VEAU

1/2 plain bagel
2 tablespoons milk
1 pound ground veal
1 egg, beaten
Dash salt
Dash freshly ground pepper
1 tablespoon vegetable oil
1/4 cup white wine
1 (8-oz.) can stewed tomatoes
2 plain bagels, sliced

Crumble 1/2 bagel. In a small bowl, soak crumbs in milk. In a medium-size bowl, combine veal with egg. Add milk-soaked crumbs, salt and pepper; blend thoroughly. Form in 4 equal-size patties. In a large skillet, heat oil. Saute patties in oil until browned on both sides. Remove and keep warm. Deglaze pan juices with wine. Add tomatoes and simmer 10 minutes. Toast 2 bagels and place 1 bagel half on each of four plates. Place 1 patty atop each bagel half and cover with sauce. (Serves 4)

REUBEN BAGEL

1 tablespoon butter
1 pumpernickel or rye bagel, sliced
1/4 pound lean corned beef
1 tablespoon Russian dressing
2 tablespoons sauerkraut, drained
2 slices Swiss cheese

Preheat oven to 350F (175C). In a small skillet, melt butter. Saute both sides of bagel halves. Place bagels, sliced-sides up, in a small baking dish. Lay corned beef across bagel halves and spread with dressing. Spread sauerkraut over corned beef and top with cheese. Bake in preheated oven 10 to 15 minutes or until cheese is melted. (Serves 1)

CAT & MOUSE BAGEL

1 (3-3/4-oz.) tin skinned boneless sardines
1 tablespoon catsup
2 tablespoons processed cheese spread
1 egg, hard-boiled
1 poppy-seed bagel, sliced

In a small bowl, mash sardines, catsup and cheese spread. Grate egg into sardine mixture; mix thoroughly. Toast bagel, then spread with sardine paste. (Serves 1)

You don't need to play shortstop to love bagels.

THE BALLPARK BAGEL

1 all-beef frankfurter   **1 tablespoon prepared mustard**
1 plain bagel, sliced   **2 tablespoons sauerkraut, drained**

Cut diagonal notches from end to end of frankfurter, cutting about 1/3 of way through. Brown frankfurter in a small skillet. As frankfurter starts to curl, pull ends together and secure with a wooden pick. Frankfurter will be bagel-shaped when cooked through. Lightly toast bagel. Spread both halves with mustard. Place frankfurter on bottom half of bagel. Top with sauerkraut and remaining bagel half. (Serves 1)

Is it like Mammela used to make? No, it's better!

CHOPPED CHICKEN LIVER SPREAD

1/2 pound chicken livers, cleaned
1 cup white wine
1 tablespoon butter or chicken fat
1 hard-boiled egg yolk
2 hard-boiled egg whites
1/2 cup finely chopped onion
1 teaspoon brandy or cognac
4 onion or rye bagels, sliced

In a small saucepan, cover chicken livers with wine. Simmer over low heat until cooked through. Drain, reserving wine broth. In a blender, puree livers and egg yolk and whites, adding 1 to 2 tablespoons of wine broth for smooth consistency. Blend in onion and brandy. Spread on bagels. (Serves 4)

BLACKENED BAGELS

These make an excellent accompaniment to any Creole or Cajun dish!

4 plain bagels, sliced
6 tablespoons butter, melted
1 teaspoon salt
1 teaspoon garlic salt
1 teaspoon onion powder
2 teaspoons paprika
1/2 teaspoon cayenne pepper
1/2 teaspoon black pepper
1/4 teaspoon dried leaf thyme
1/4 teaspoon dried leaf oregano

Place bagels, sliced-sides up, in a large baking dish. Spread 5 tablespoons butter on bagels. In a small bowl, combine salt, garlic, onion powder, paprika, cayenne pepper, black pepper, thyme and oregano; mix well. Sprinkle powder over bagels. Pat on by hand until powder forms a heavy crust. Dot with remaining 1 tablespoon of butter. Broil in toaster oven or broiler. (Serves 4)

BAGELS JAMBALAYA

In Louisiana this is traditionally made with shrimp, but it's also a good way to use up leftover poultry or ham.

2 plain bagels
1 slice bacon, diced
1/2 small onion, chopped
2 teaspoons all-purpose flour
2 tomatoes, peeled, seeded
1/2 green bell pepper, diced
1/4 cup water
1-1/2 cups cooked rice
1 cup coarsely chopped cooked shrimp
1 (4-inch) chunk hot sausage, cut in rounds
1 tablespoon chopped fresh parsley
Pinch thyme

Slice bagels horizontally in thirds and toast lightly. Cut toasted bagel slices in thin strips. In a medium-size saucepan, saute bacon. Add onion and saute until onion is golden. Blend in flour. Stir in tomatoes, bell pepper and water; bring to a boil. Stir in rice, shrimp, sausage, parsley and thyme, stirring constantly. Reduce heat to simmer. Cook 8 minutes, stirring constantly. Place bagel strips on a platter and top with sauce. (Serves 2)

BAYOU BAGEL BOATS

4 sesame bagels, sliced
7 tablespoons butter or margarine
1 cup shelled deveined raw shrimp, coarsely chopped
1/2 cup crab meat
2 tablespoons finely chopped onion
2 tablespoons finely chopped green bell pepper
1/2 cup dry sherry
3 tablespoons all-purpose flour
1-1/2 cups milk
Dash salt
Dash pepper
1/4 cup shredded Gruyère cheese
Paprika

Preheat oven to 400F (205C). Butter 4 ramekins or small baking dishes. Make hollows in bagels to form 8 "boats." Butter insides of "boats" with 2 tablespoons of butter. Place 2 bagel halves, sliced-sides up, in each ramekin. In a large skillet, melt 2 tablespoons of butter. Add seafood, onion and bell pepper. Cook 2 to 3 minutes or until bell pepper has wilted. Add sherry, stirring gently. Remove from heat. In a small saucepan, melt remaining 3 tablespoons of butter. Add flour gradually, stirring with a fork or wire whisk until fully blended. In another small saucepan, heat milk just to boiling and add to butter mixture; stir until thick and smooth. Add sauce, salt and pepper to seafood mixture; stir lightly to mix. Spoon into "boats." Sprinkle with cheese and dust with paprika. Bake in preheated oven 10 minutes. (Serves 4)

Break out the Dixieland jazz, bite into these and get that French Quarter feeling.

BAGEL à l'ORANGE

2 tablespoons orange marmalade
2 tablespoons Grand Marnier
1 cinnamon-raisin bagel, sliced

In a custard cup, mix marmalade with 1 teaspoon of Grand Marnier. Pour remaining Grand Marnier into a shallow dish. Soak bagel halves in Grand Marnier 1/2 hour. Toast bagel lightly. Spread marmalade mixture on bagel. Toast until marmalade is piping hot. (Serves 1)

You're sure to agree our version beats toast and jam.

APPLE BAGELS à la MODE

1 large apple
1 tablespoon butter
2 tablespoons sugar
3 tablespoons white rum
1 cinnamon-raisin bagel, sliced
2 scoops French vanilla ice cream
1 teaspoon ground cinnamon

Core and peel apple. Slice vertically in thin slices. Melt butter in a medium-size skillet. Cook apple slices about 5 minutes, stirring carefully so slices don't break. Add sugar and cook 5 minutes, stirring just enough to blend sugar with pan juices. Remove from heat, add rum and flambé. Toast bagel. Place 1 bagel half in each of 2 dessert dishes. Spoon apple slices over bagel half. Top each with 1 scoop of ice cream. Dust with cinnamon. Pour sauce over ice cream. (Serves 2)

It's hot and cold and every bite is scrumptious.

BAGEL PUDDING

A beloved dessert gets a new-fangled design and a tastier taste.

1 cup dry cinnamon-raisin bagel cubes
1-1/2 cups scalded milk
2 eggs, slightly beaten
1/2 cup sugar
1/2 cup seedless raisins
2 tablespoons butter, softened
1 teaspoon ground cinnamon
1/2 teaspoon ground nutmeg

In a medium-size bowl, soak bagel cubes in milk about 20 minutes. Butter a medium-size baking dish. Preheat oven to 375F (190C). Add eggs and sugar to bagel cubes, stirring until sugar dissolves. Add remaining ingredients and pour into buttered dish. Set dish in a pan of hot water. Bake in preheated oven about 1/2 hour or until a knife inserted near edge comes out clean. Serve chilled or at room temperature. (Serves 4 to 6)

TIPSY TRIFLE

Here's a dessert to loosen even the stiffest British upper lip!

1 cup medium-dry or sweet sherry
4 cinnamon-raisin bagels, sliced
1 cup prepared custard sauce
1/2 cup raspberry preserves
1 cup whipped cream
1/4 cup blanched sliced almonds, lightly toasted

Pour sherry into a shallow flat-bottomed glass dish. Pierce each bagel half several times and place, sliced-side down, in sherry. Soak at least 1/2 hour. Spoon 1 tablespoon of sauce in center of each of 4 deep dessert dishes. Spread each bagel half with raspberry preserves. Place 1 bagel half, sliced-side up, in each desert dish. Drizzle with several tablespoons of sauce. Top with remaining bagel halves, sliced-sides down. Pour remaining sauce over bagels. Top with whipped cream and almonds. (Serves 4)

MERRY-GO-ROUND BAGEL

1 plain or cinnamon-raisin bagel, sliced
1/2 cup marshmallow spread
Multicolored "jimmies" or sprinkles
2 tablespoons flaked coconut
6 animal crackers

Lightly toast each bagel half; cool. Spread each bagel half generously with marshmallow spread. Sprinkle with coconut flakes and gently press flakes so they will stick. Sprinkle "jimmies" over coconut. To decorate, place 3 animal crackers in an upright position on each bagel half. (Serves 2)

ZUPPA INGLESE

This beloved dessert from Italy is easy to make, delicious and especially adaptable for bagel mavens!

4 cinnamon-raisin bagels
1/2 cup dark rum
1/2 ounce unsweetened chocolate, grated
1 cup homemade or prepared custard
1 (16-oz.) can chocolate frosting

Slice each bagel in thirds horizontally. Prick bagel slices several times with a fork. Pour rum into a medium-size dish; soak bagels in rum. Combine chocolate with 1/3 of custard. Place 1 bagel slice on each of 4 dessert plates. Spread with 1/2 of remaining plain custard. Top each with another bagel slice. Spread with chocolate custard. Top with remaining bagel slices and spread with remaining plain custard. Chill overnight. To serve, frost sides of each "cake" with chocolate frosting. (Serves 4)

HOT FUDGE BAGEL SUPREME

1 cinnamon-raisin bagel, sliced
2 teaspoons dark creme de cocoa
1 scoop vanilla ice cream
3 tablespoons hot fudge sauce
2 teaspoons chopped walnuts
Dab whipped cream
2 maraschino cherries

Toast bagel and prick both halves with a fork. In a shallow dish, soak bagel halves in creme de cocoa 15 minutes. Put 1 bagel half, sliced-side up, in a dessert dish. Top with ice cream, then second bagel half, sliced-side down. Heat fudge topping. Pour over bagel. Top with nuts, whipped cream and cherries. (Serves 1)

If you're counting calories, stop counting and start enjoying!

MAIL-ORDER DIRECTORY

No matter where you live or travel in the United States, it's always possible to have your breakfast bagel. There are companies that will ship bagels, as well as smoked salmon, for overnight delivery anyplace in America. In addition to ordering bagels and lox by mail, you can also order various bagel toppings, cookware to make bagels at home, and knives and gadgets to use in serving and cutting bagels. Here is a list of companies that will fulfill the whims, as well as the needs, of bagelmaniacs.

◆

A Taste of Philadelphia
672 Colwell Rd.
Woodlyn, PA 19094
1-215-328-5060

On special request, this company will air-mail fresh Philadelphia-baked bagels, along with lox, smoked salmon, etc. They also deliver such Philly-food favorites as hoagies, cheese steaks, tastycakes, cinnamon buns and scrapple.

◆

H & H Bagels
2239 Broadway
New York, NY 10023
1-800-NY-BAGEL
(In New York State including Manhattan call: 1-800-882-2435)

One of the finest bagel bakeries in New York City, H & H will express mail fresh bagels all over the country. Their bagels are certified by the Kosher Supervision Service, and come in such varieties as onion, cinnamon-raisin, sourdough, garlic, pumpernickel, sesame and poppy seed, as well as plain. There is a minimum order of three dozen, and you must call by 10 a.m. for next-day delivery. Often cited as "the best bagel bakery" in Manhattan, H & H pops out more than 50,000 bagels a day. No wonder their mail order slogan is "You will be in Heaven. . . . Share them!"

The Wooden Spoon
Route 6
Mahopac, NY 10541
1-800-431-2207
(In New York State call collect: 0-914-628-3747)

An acrylic bagel vise that can be purchased with or without a serrated knife is available from this catalog that features a dazzling array of kitchen gadgets and cooking tools. Everything you ever dreamed of to cook with, plus many things you didn't know existed, make this catalog a food lover's delight.

◆

Oak & Iron
2700 Commerce St.
La Crosse, WI
1-800-356-5432
(In Wisconsin call: 1-800-362-6060)

Oak & Iron offers a terrific bagel-cutting device that consists of a red oak block with a copper-lined inset where you place the bagel. The inset makes it easier to cut the bagel in practically perfect halves! Available with or without a serrated stainless steel knife.

Zabar's
2245 Broadway
New York, NY 10024
1-212-787-2000
1-800-221-3347

Zabar's is one of New York City's most significant landmarks; it's to food what Bloomingdale's is to clothes. No wonder it's been featured in so many Woody Allen movies! Gourmets and cooks find their every need fulfilled at Zabar's, which aptly calls itself a "gourmet emporium." There are over 100 different kinds of cheese, an abundance of smoked fish, all kinds of kitchen gadgets and tools (at often hard-to-beat prices), as well as the customary delicatessen food stuffs. Zabar's will ship lox and other varieties of smoked salmon anywhere in the United States for an extra charge. Despite the gamut and quality of the goods, Zabar's is not over-priced. In fact. there are often sales and price wars with Macy's Cellar on such high-ticket items as caviar and smoked salmon that result in super-savings for the consumer. A recent holiday sale featured a pound of pre-sliced Scottish salmon for as low as $14.95. The Zabar's experience is something that must be personally witnessed to be fully appreciated, but for those outside New York City, a catalog captures some of the epicurean delights to be found here.

Russ and Daughters
179 East Houston St.
New York, NY 10002
1-212-475-4880

Even if the address isn't Park Avenue, the fish here is high-quality and fancy enough to please the most persnickety gourmets. There are all kinds of fish delicacies in this well-stocked appetizing store. The smoked Gaspé salmon is sliced and placed back on its skin. There are also lake sturgeon, pickled herring, fresh caviar and lox. Fancy coffees, nuts and candies are also available in this family-owned and operated shop that's been around for several generations. Minimum mail order is $100.00.

Bridge Company
212 East 52nd St.
New York, NY 10022
1-212-688-4220

A specialty shop with over 40,000 items that services the professional as well as the non-pro baker and cook. They offer many utensils and serving pieces that enhance bagel baking and serving. Julia Child is one of its many famed customers.

Williams-Sonoma
Mail Order Department
P.O. Box 7456
San Francisco, CA 94120-7456
1-415-421-4242

Williams-Sonoma is probably the "haute" catalog for all kinds of cooks. In addition to traditional wares, it features items specially designed for W-S that can't be found anywhere else. Their selection of baking pans and chef's knives suitable for slicing bagels are bound to please even the most demanding bagel buff.

Hammacher Schlemmer
147 East 57th St.
New York, NY 10022
1-800-543-3366

A self-adjusting wide-mouth toaster, that can accommodate the largest bagel or bagel half, is just one of the many items in this catalog of all kinds of gadgets and electronic contraptions and thingamajigs. This is truly a gadget addict's paradise, and it's fun just to browse the pages.

◆

Josephson's Smokehouse and Dock
106 Marine Dr.
Astoria, OR 97103
1-800-772-3474
(In Oregon call
1-800-828- 3474)

This company offers top-quality smoked sockeye salmon cured the Swedish way. It's cold smoked with alder-wood, and comes moist, medium or hard smoked. Canned seafood and gift packages also available.

Caviarteria, Inc.
29 East 60th St.
New York, NY 10022
1-800-4-CAVIAR

All varieties of smoked salmon, plus gravlax, which a company spokesperson recommended as "scrumptious on a freshly baked bagel," can be found here, along with all kinds of Russian and American caviar, German hams and an assortment of pâtés.

◆

Norm Thompson
P.O. Box 3999
Portland, OR 97208
1-800-547-1160

In addition to clothing, footwear, gift items and novelties, this company also offers specialty foods and impressive food gift packs. Bagelmaniacs will appreciate their smoked salmon pâté, as well as the customary smoked salmon fillets. Norm Thompson also has such gourmet goods as French mints, old-world beer bread, thin ginger wafers and Oregon marionberry syrup for round-the-world eating.

Barney Greengrass
541 Amsterdam Avenue
New York, NY 10024
1-212-724-4707

This appetizer store on the Upper West Side of Manhattan enjoys a fine reputation for its smoked fish. They will UPS mail special gift packages of bagels, smoked fish, cream and other kinds of cheeses all over the country.

◆

Colonial Garden Kitchens
Unique Merchandise Mart
Building 66
Hanover, PA 17333
1-800-621-5800
(In Illinois, call:
1-800-972-5855)

This company's version of a bagel cutter is acrylic with a polyethylene cutting block on the bottom that won't damage your knife. Other special items in this catalog of creative cooking utensils include a fat-free loaf pan for ungreasy meatloaf, artichoke serving plates, a microwave safety meter and a zabaglione pot. A wealth of baking tools are also offered.

**Hegg and Hegg Smoked
  Salmon, Inc.
801 Marine Dr.
Port Angeles, WA 98362
1-800-435-3474
(In Washington State call:
1- 206-457-3344)**

For over 35 years, this company has been selling smoked salmon and other smoked fish, as well as canned seafood, through the mails. They offer the traditional smoked salmon, such as nova, but also sell their own Western red smoked salmon, which is sockeye from Puget Sound. Other Hegg and Hegg delectables are smoked and fresh tiny baby shrimp, smoked tuna, smoked sturgeon, shad roe, as well as an entire line of no-salt smoked products. (Yes, Virginia, you can still have smoked salmon on your salt-free diet!) Delivery is guaranteed on all items, and prices for smoked salmon are incredibly low. For example, a side of smoked salmon, which weighs about 2 pounds, is $18.75 west of the Rockies and $21.00 east of the Rockies. An entire smoked salmon, which weighs about 4 pounds, goes for $34.00 west of the Rockies and $38.00 east of the Rockies. All kinds of gift packages available.

◆

**Balducci's
334 East 11th Street
New York, NY 10003-7426
1-800-822-1444
(In New York State call:
1-800-247-2450)**

Balducci's, in the heart of Greenwich Village in Manhattan, ranks as another of the city's fine gourmet food stores. They will overnight mail a minimum order of $20 worth of bagels, which amounts to roughly 40 bagels. For delicious bagel accompaniments, Balducci's mails out six different kinds of smoked salmon (Norwegian, Scotch, Irish, Nova, Eastern Nova, Western Nova), a variety of cream cheeses, including one with caviar, and butter logs from different regions of the U.S. and the world. A catalogue is $3.00, which is credited towards your order and informs foodlovers of the entire mouth-watering display here.

**Pfaelzer Brothers
16W347 83rd St.
Burr Ridge, IL 60521
1-800-621-0226
(Illinois residents call collect:
0-312-325-9700)**

Sides of smoked Irish and Scotch salmon can be ordered from this company to complement bagels, as well as various pâtés and crocks of cheese. Pfaelzer Brothers features a mouth-watering array of meats, fish, poultry, cheese and desserts, and their catalog alone is enough to make anyone salivate. They are especially good at solving the too-busy-to-cook dilemma, since they deliver gourmet meals such as Beef Wellington and Crown Roast of Pork, ready to be popped into the oven and served. For those with a sweet tooth, there are Pfaelzer's own secret-recipe Pina Colada Cake, a Karisma Mousse Cake that looks positively sinful and a Chocolate Snack Pak for chocoholics.

◆

The Gourmet Pantry
400 McGuinness Blvd.
Brooklyn, NY 11222
1-718-383-5314

Smoked salmon can be ordered from this company, as well as other delicacies such as cheeses, nuts, cookies, fruits and exotic fowl. They have toy and gift items in their catalogs.

◆

Weather Vane Lobster
Company
62 Badgers Island
Kittery, ME 03904
1-800-343-4000

Smoked salmon is available here along with other fresh seafood, such as lobster, clams and oysters, salt codfish and mackerel. A free catalog details their selection of fish specialties.

◆

S.E.Rykoff & Co.
P.O. Box 21467
Los Angeles, CA 90021
1-800-421-9873

Since 1911, this West Coast firm has been catering to bagel addicts and epicures everywhere with their smoked salmon and other food items. Cooking tools and paper products are also available.

MAIL-ORDER BAGEL BRIDE

Shipping bagels by mail has become so popular that the custom even made the movies. In the film *Heartburn,* the character of Rachel Samstat is having a serious case of cold feet about marrying writer Mark Foreman and moving from New York to Washington, D.C.

"You can't even get a decent bagel in Washington," she wails to a Manhattan editor friend.

"I'll send them to you Federal Express," he replies. That promise may have been the turning point, because shortly thereafter, Rachel is finally able to emerge from the bedroom and march down the aisle to her long-waiting groom.

Recipe Index